"*In God's Good Image* is an invita[tion]
of the creator God in the multitudes around us, even in those
so unlike us. J. W. Buck walks readers through the narrative
of Scripture to encourage us to become acquainted with our
own cultural heritage. In doing so, we can become more
spacious, welcoming people who see the cultural other as our
beloved neighbor."

JENAI AUMAN, author of *Othered: Finding Belonging with the God Who Pursues the Hurt, Harmed, and Marginalized*

"Who defines and clarifies our cultural identity? J. W. Buck
explores this question and many others in this thoughtful and
expansive treatise on the meaning and purpose of our cultural
identities. With the premise that all cultures possess God-given
dignity and beauty, Buck deftly explains how we may love one
another well amid the cultural mosaic in our societies. Ending
with practical takeaways, this book is a must-read and a valu-
able reference for understanding the sacredness, meaning, and
role of our cultural identities."

PRASANTA VERMA, MPH, MBA, speaker, public health professional, and author of *Beyond Ethnic Loneliness: The Pain of Marginalization and the Path to Belonging*

"The globalization of our world has caused cultures to collide,
cultural stories once forgotten to be told, cultural sins to be
repented of, and cultural flourishing to be celebrated. *In God's
Good Image* leads the reader on a journey that emphatically
demonstrates that Jesus deeply cares for and died for peoples
and cultures around the world and across time. J. W. Buck
doesn't shy away from difficult scripture passages about the
destruction of peoples and cultures but leans into the good and
redeeming story of Jesus, the cross, and New Creation."

ERNESTO DUKE, president of Eternity College

IN GOD'S GOOD IMAGE

IN

How Jesus Dignifies, Shapes, and

GOD'S

Confronts Our Cultural Identities

GOOD

J. W. BUCK

IMAGE

HERALD
P R E S S

Harrisonburg, Virginia

Herald Press
PO Box 866, Harrisonburg, Virginia 22803
www.HeraldPress.com

Library of Congress Cataloging-in-Publication Data
Names: Buck, J. W. (Joshua W.), author.
Title: In God's good image : how Jesus dignifies, shapes, and confronts our
    cultural identities / J.W. Buck.
Description: Harrisonburg, Virginia : Herald Press, [2024] | Includes
    bibliographical references.
Identifiers: LCCN 2024031686 (print) | LCCN 2024031687 (ebook) | ISBN
    9781513813660 (paperback) | ISBN 9781513813677 (hardcover) | ISBN
    9781513813684 (ebook)
Subjects: LCSH: Jesus Christ--Character. | Identification (Religion) |
    Christian life. | BISAC: RELIGION / Christian Living / Social Issues |
    RELIGION / Christian Living / Personal Growth
Classification: LCC BT304 .B74 2024 (print) | LCC BT304 (ebook) | DDC
    232.9--dc23/eng/20240823
LC record available at https://lccn.loc.gov/2024031686
LC ebook record available at https://lccn.loc.gov/2024031687

Permission to use the three Jesus icons on pages 44, 46, and 47 have been given by the digital
artist Josue Carballo-Huertas.

Study guides are available for many Herald Press titles at www.HeraldPress.com.

IN GOD'S GOOD IMAGE
© 2024 by Herald Press, Harrisonburg, Virginia 22803. 800-245-7894. All rights reserved.
Library of Congress Control Number: 2024031686
International Standard Book Number: 978-1-5138-1366-0 (paperback);
    978-1-5138-1367-7 (hardcover); 978-1-5138-1368-4 (ebook)
Printed in United States of America
Cover resources: melitas / iStock / Getty Images Plus; aga7ta / iStock / Getty Images Plus;
    zenstock / iStock / Getty Images Plus; sensationaldesign / iStock / Getty Images Plus

Scripture quotations are from New Revised Standard Version Updated Edition. Copyright
© 2021 National Council of the Churches of Christ in the United States of America. Used by
permission. All rights reserved worldwide. Scripture quotations marked (EHV) are from the
Holy Bible, Evangelical Heritage Version® (EHV®) © 2019 Wartburg Project, Inc. All rights
reserved. Used by permission. Scripture quotations marked (NIV) are taken from the Holy
Bible, New International Version®, NIV®. Copyright © 1973, 1978, 1984, 2011 by Biblica,
Inc.® Used by permission of Zondervan. All rights reserved worldwide. www.zondervan.com
The "NIV" and "New International Version" are trademarks registered in the United States
Patent and Trademark Office by Biblica, Inc.®

28 27 26 25 24   10 9 8 7 6 5 4 3 2 1

To my wife and children:

*Sarswatie Rampersaud, Aahana Rampersaud,
Anaia Rose, and Azariah Emory*

Thank you for being my daily teachers.

CONTENTS

FOREWORD

I was raised in two distinctly different geographic locations: a small town in northern New Mexico and urban Honolulu. Although each place is distinct in so many ways, my two homes share certain similarities. Namely, both places have communities of people from different cultural backgrounds, each with their own rich heritage, languages, history, and traditions. Over the years, as I traversed back and forth from one place to the other, the interactions I had with classmates and friends in my community introduced me to the complex concept of culture and the notion that people view the world differently. My own multicultural upbringing in these formative years sparked my curiosities about cultures, eventually leading me to my academic career as a professor of intercultural studies.

I don't think my story is unique. My hunch is that each reader of this book has also been shaped through interactions with others in this ever-changing and interconnected world. We all hail from places where there is no longer just one cultural narrative—if there was ever one at all. Globalization and migration have created spaces in which people with nuanced and layered identities interact daily.

And yet, recognizing that the world is culturally diverse is not enough. We must also do the hard work of understanding our own cultural identities, to deepen an understanding of ourselves, of others, and of God.

J. W. Buck has written a book that will help you do just that.

I first met J. W. (whom I know as Josh) when he started his PhD in intercultural studies at Biola University. As the doctoral program director, I was Josh's advisor, and I eventually went on to serve as his dissertation chair. I was so pleased when I learned that he was writing this book. In its pages, it is evident that he has combined his deep love for people and for God with his own curiosities about cultures. Josh has extensive personal and professional experiences living and working in multicultural settings, which positions him well to write this book.

But beyond seeing a student flourish in his postdoctoral years, it is also satisfying to read a book that is needed at this very time; a time when a disregard for understanding others seems to dominate interactions. *In God's Good Image* invites the reader on a journey of understanding. It confronts the notion that identities are monolithic and that worldviews are limited to dominant perspectives. By focusing on culture through the lens of the Old and New Testaments, Josh has established a foundation for readers to understand cultures through stories in Scripture. He also helpfully provides a section in the book for individuals, churches, and pastors to reflect and consider how they might apply the principles from the book in their personal and professional lives. I would add that academics, both students and faculty, will benefit from using this book in their respective courses.

As you dive into this book, I encourage you to read with an open mind and reflective heart. Sit with God to understand your own story and how God has shaped you. In doing so, you will gain a deeper connection with those in your community, church, and beyond.

—Jamie N. Sanchez, PhD
Associate professor in intercultural studies,
Talbot School of Theology at Biola University

INTRODUCTION

In 2016, I was sitting in a doctoral class called social anthro-pology. I was one of fifteen students from across the world trying to better understand how faith and culture intersect. Our professor had asked us to prepare a fifteen-minute pre-sentation about the intersection between our cultural identity and the Christian faith, and that day it was my turn to present.

In my short speech, I opened with the Dutch roots of my family as we migrated from the Netherlands to Maine. From there, the Bucks migrated slowly down to Texas over the course of about fifty years. I talked about what it was like growing up within a majority white area while attending evangelical reformed Anglo-Saxon churches. A theme in the cultural story line was that I did not think about my cultural identity very much at all. I was formed within majority culture spaces where my home culture was not greatly challenged or disputed. I grew up as a white American in a dominant white American culture.

To end the presentation, I talked about how it took several cross-cultural experiences, meeting my Indo-Guyanese wife, and living in a Mexican American immigrant community to begin reflecting on my own cultural identity. "I didn't really consider that Christianity was not of European origin until

I attended Bible college," I said. "At that point, I realized Jesus was Jewish. It took me a while to realize that European people were invited into the story of God and not the center of God's story." I concluded by letting the class know that I was very much in the process of growing in my Christian cultural identity.

With my presentation behind me, I settled comfortably in the second-to-last row, excited to hear the other students. The next person to present was a twenty-seven-year-old second-generation Latina student named Sofia.[1] Sofia opened by saying she grew up in a bilingual home in East Los Angeles. She then talked about her spiritual formation in Pentecostal Hispanic church spaces as a youth.

About five minutes into the presentation, Sofia paused and became emotional. We all felt it in the room. She was trying not to cry. In a compassionate voice, our professor told Sofia to take a minute. "No, I'm okay," Sofia said. After a long pause, she continued, saying, "It has been hard to figure out my cultural identity. I feel caught between generations in my church, and I'm trying to navigate where I fit in. After high school, I attended a mostly white Christian university for my undergraduate degree. It was culture shock for me. I never felt so alone, and I didn't realize how hard it would be as a cultural minority in a space that was supposed to be accepting of my culture. I'm still discerning what it means to be a Christian while at the same time to be comfortable in my own cultural identity. I'm learning it is hard to be a cultural minority in Christian spaces." Sofia then reflected on the challenge of going back into her home church as a second-generation Latina who did not quite fit in anymore. She felt caught between the dominant white Christian culture and the divide between generations within her church. Sofia ended by explaining that she was considering finding a new church community where she could begin to rethink her own cultural heritage as she follows Jesus. She ended by seamlessly weaving the course content into her own story.

Later that day, I reflected on why hers was such a memorable presentation. Sofia captured in a very eloquent way the journey of discovering that she was a cultural minority within the Christian college she attended. She expressed so much pain and turmoil in her journey. Though I had heard many of the same things from friends and fellow church members, her story stuck with me.

It was also glaringly apparent how different my own cultural narrative and faith formation had been. I grew up to discover I was a majority culture Christian—it did not come naturally for me to think about my cultural identity. In contrast, Sofia grew up to realize that she was an ethnic minority in Christian spaces and that she had always been very aware of her cultural identity. While I expressed a measure of tension in my cultural narrative, I did not harbor deep pain like Sofia did. I was speaking about my faith and cultural identity from a dominant culture perspective. Sofia was speaking about the same topics in light of growing up in a Mexican American community and sifting through the experiences of being a second-generation immigrant.

While we served the same God, believed in the same gospel, read the same Bible, were in the same class, lived in the same city, and shared in a common humanity, we were developing our cultural identities from very different places. Yet as the many presentations in our class had made clear, everyone was trying to find their cultural clarity in Jesus. This brings us to the crossroads of this book: Amid the many different cultural stories we inhabit, we must all develop our cultural identity in

Jesus Christ. This book is a journey toward Jesus as the One who can enlighten our cultural path.

FOLLOWING JESUS FROM OUR CULTURAL LOCATION

While we all have vastly different cultural starting points, Jesus must be the center in our understanding of culture. By surveying the Scriptures, we will learn that the chief aim of all people is to worship Jesus and love those around us. For majority culture Christians, we follow Jesus by embracing a posture of cultural humility toward others. We love our neighbor by setting aside our own cultural preferences to create space for others. Jesus teaches us to value the cultural identity in others—especially if they are different! For minority culture Christians, we will discover that God stands in solidarity with those who have suffered cultural harms. Our scriptural survey will show that Jesus especially dignifies minority culture by living as a minority Hebrew under the poverty line in occupied territory. We will learn from the many passages we study that God has made all people in the beautiful image of God in order to display Christ from within our unique ways of life.

Each section of this book is part of a journey in which the story of God speaks to both majority and minority culture Christians. No matter where you come from and no matter how complex your cultural narrative, the Scriptures point to the One who embodied a minority Jewish culture to shape your cultural identity!

BOOK OVERVIEW

This book explores the intersection between Jesus and our cultural location. We will traverse the Scriptures to discern how Jesus Christ wants us to dignify, shape, and confront our cultural upbringing.

Throughout this book, I weave in stories from my own cultural formation as someone who loves multicultural settings, planted a multicultural church, has lived oversees, has co-led diverse organizations, and has a multiethnic family. Even amid these important experiences, I had further questions about the intersection of faith, culture, and cultural identity. For this reason, I obtained a PhD in intercultural studies. This book weaves in the knowledge and insights gained over the course of my doctoral studies.

Does this mean I'm an expert? No. I have made lots of mistakes as a white Christian leader. A lot. I have had to ask for forgiveness many times. There are times I've not been sensitive to those from different cultural backgrounds. I have many cultural blind spots I'm still trying to account for. I have failed over and over, both personally and professionally, because of my lack of cultural understanding. While writing this book, I had moments of confession before God knowing that I'm still trying to live up to the standard that Jesus has set for us. I am trying, every day, to live into the truths that I draw out across this book. By highlighting a range of personal experiences, I hope to humanize our collective journey toward the better world that God wants us to create.

Throughout the book (and in the appendix), you'll find places to reflect on your own identity and your perception of other people's identities and cultural contexts. I especially encourage other majority culture readers to engage this book with cultural humility, a willingness to confess and seek forgiveness when you fail, and to not let the fear of failure keep you from walking down this road. It all starts with better understanding ourselves, Scripture, and how Jesus has the power to form and inform our cultural identities.

Part 1

JESUS-CENTERED IDENTITY

1

THE JEWISH JESUS

Main point

▶ The cultural Christ liberates us to discover our true cultural identity.

I grew up in a small town called Enumclaw, outside of Seattle, Washington. When I was a child, we attended a small Reformed church of about fifty people. I grew close with a few of the pastor's kids who were my age, and about once a month my mother dropped me off at their house to play. We played with bees, annoyed the girls, ate tons of food, and lost track of time playing daylong board games. One day we were running up and down the hallway that connected the kitchen to the backyard. From a distant room, my friend's mom yelled, "Stop running!" I froze in the hallway, hoping I wouldn't get in trouble. Trying to catch my breath, I looked to the wall on my right. There hung a very famous painting, Warner Sallman's *Head of Christ*.

I stared at this painting for what seemed like five minutes but was probably ten seconds. A light was beaming down on his serious resting face, his eyes looked outward and up, and he wore an angelic white robe. These elements gave the painting a religious feel. Jesus had white skin and European facial features—a pointy, narrow nose; blue eyes; defined small lips; high cheekbones; and a light brown beard. In the painting, his brownish blond hair was flowing onto his shoulders from his head. The image felt sacred. This was the Messiah who came to forgive us of our sins. This was the leader my parents taught me to trust and follow with all my life. The fact that Jesus was white didn't feel wrong or right. It simply was the "truth" I saw in the painting.[1]

This was not the last time in my childhood that I encountered white Jesus. While reading Christian books and visiting various churches over the years, this same white version of Jesus appeared in different ways. In this white Jesus, I saw my own culture. I saw a middle-aged version of myself. I saw a representation of my family, my culture, and my way of life. It never occurred to me that Jesus was actually Jewish and came from a very different cultural background from what I knew. Maybe I missed that Sunday school lesson.

SPANISH IN HEAVEN

When my sister Shelby and I became teens, my parents decided to switch churches to one with more kids our age. The church that we joined did have more kids, and it also did lots of missions work around the world. When I was fifteen years old, my mother decided we would all go on a short-term mission trip to Mexico. We raised some money, went through training, and set off to serve at an orphanage for a week. It was a profound experience for me to live and breathe outside of American culture. Even though the orphanage staff made those of us from the United States very comfortable, it was still jarring for me to serve in an environment where I was in the minority.

On Sunday, we went to a small church at the orphanage, and I found myself culturally uncomfortable at church for the first time in my life. Most of the church service was in Spanish, and I struggled to read the lyrics and understand what was going on. The sermon was delivered in Spanish, so we wore headsets to hear the translation. The pastor was preaching on the book of Revelation. While I don't remember the sermon, I do remember one very cunning joke he told. "When we get to the presence of Jesus, God will wipe away every tear from our eyes!" he said in Spanish. "There will be no more pain or sorrow. And no one will force us to speak English anymore. Everyone here knows we will be speaking God's language in heaven—Spanish!"

A rolling laughter overcame the room as the Spanish speakers broke out in a cheer. After the translation came into our headsets, a slightly less gregarious and more nervous laughter set in from those of us who spoke only English. We smiled and laughed, but it was uncomfortable. The amazing joke had made me laugh, but in the middle of my smile, I began to feel offended. I thought to myself, "Wait a minute—we won't be speaking Spanish in heaven; we'll be speaking English. Why would we be speaking Spanish in heaven?"

My cultural assumption that God endorsed white English-speaking culture was being challenged by a pastor in Mexico. For the first time in my life, I had to consider my own cultural identity. But this was just the beginning of God challenging the false cultural and biblical assumptions I grew up believing.

JESUS IN YOUR IMAGE

The anthropologist Zora Neale Hurston once said, "Gods always behave like the people who make them."[2] I want you to pause to think about what this means. While doing research in the Caribbean and the American South, Hurston discovered a common tendency among religious people. She found that humans tend to fashion the gods they serve in their own image. The local deities she studied tended to talk, act, and think like the people who served them. This applies to Christianity too. Christians often imagine a God who looks, dresses, thinks, talks, and acts like they do. In fact, regardless of where you are in the world, you probably tend to project your own cultural identity on Jesus, too—even if just subconsciously.

Go online and search for different images of Jesus from around the world. Jesus will look different according to who has created the art. Filipinos end up sculpting a Filipino Jesus. Kenyans paint a Kenyan Jesus. Guatemalans draw a Guatemalan Jesus. Native Americans create a Jesus specific to their various contexts. White people create a white Jesus. Is this all bad? No. There is beauty in seeing Jesus in all cultures—the apostle Paul teaches us in Colossians that "Christ is all and in all" (Colossians 3:11). This verse means, among other things, that Christ is reflected across cultures in myriad ways. God has dignified all people by creating all people in the image of God.

For some people groups, their local artwork of Jesus is an act of resistance to the violent white Jesus that has been imposed on them. For the communities across the world that have been taught that Jesus is white, that Christianity is a European religion, or that Jesus wants you to throw away your cultural identity, it is important to reimagine a Jesus who honors your own skin and way of life!

Amid these strengths, there are some dangers to projecting our own cultures onto Jesus. First, when we project our own cultural identity on Jesus, we wash away the ethnic and cultural identity of Jesus. We won't understand Jesus to be a

Jewish first-century Palestinian man, and that's an important part of his identity. Second, when we translate Jesus into our own image, we are less likely to confront our sin and our cultural blind spots. We won't see Jesus as an outsider to our own culture who can come in to help us navigate the areas where we are culturally blind. Third, when a majority culture people create Jesus in their image, they will expect others to accept and follow their version of Jesus—and become just like them. If Jesus is just like most people in an area, then the cultural outsiders will feel the pressure to live, think, and act differently. It is therefore especially dangerous for any majority culture Christian to create Jesus in their image. We end up forcing others to follow our version of Jesus in the world.

THE JEWISH JESUS

So what is the solution? We must recover the cultural Christ who made each person in the very good image of God. Instead of seeing God as a blank slate on which we project our own culture, we must rediscover the Jewish Jesus. It matters that Jesus read Hebrew and spoke Aramaic and Greek. Jesus grew up in a small Jewish town called Nazareth and conformed to the cultural customs of his time. God's Son grew up as a cultural minority who experienced poverty and suffered as a member of an occupied people. We must accept salvation from the One who embodied the very nature of God through the everyday customs of the Hebrew people. We will find that the purpose of every person is to worship and love this Jewish Messiah.

Our aim, regardless of how we currently see Jesus, is to rediscover the cultural Christ from the text of Scripture.[3] In Jesus Christ we will find a God who dignifies and challenges our cultural identity. We will discover a God who made each person in God's image to bear the mark of the divine from their unique cultural location. We will discover a gospel that both validates and confronts each local culture of the world. We must open our own cultural formation to the Christ who bled from Jewish skin to offer salvation beyond Israel. It is only because of the Jewish Jesus that we are saved, and it is only through this same Jesus that we can form our cultural identities in the world.[4]

2

A SACRED
CULTURAL IDENTITY

Main point
▶ God created all aspects of our cultural
identity to be sacred.

A few years back, I met regularly with a new Christian in his early twenties named Angel Fletes. We would talk about his dating experiences, how things were going at work, and how he was navigating a challenging family situation. One area we discussed in detail was his cultural identity. Angel was a third-generation Mexican American, had three siblings, and was raised by his mother. He had recently begun following Jesus and had decided to get more serious about church and reading the Scriptures.

During our first meeting I asked, "Could you tell me about the impact your cultural identity has on your faith?" This was a new question for Angel to explore. "No one has ever asked me about the connection between my religion and culture," he said. "I assumed my culture wouldn't be a big part of Christianity." I explained how exploring one's upbringing is an important part of the growth process as a Christian. After we talked for a few hours about how he could begin to think about this new idea, I said, "Here is your homework for the week. I want you to find some resources on cultural identity. Look for some direction from your social media feed, find some articles on some online magazines, or find some You-Tubers. Try to find some themes in what you are seeing." Angel left excited for this slightly strange assignment.

The next week I asked what he had found and what themes he had seen. Angel looked at me and said, "It was mostly self-focused . . . it was about the individual. Lots of language about your 'true self' and 'finding who you are.' A phrase that kept coming up is 'your truth' and 'your story.' I found a lot of how-to guides about developing cultural identity. I found some great stuff about how to be more culturally intelligent in situations. That was probably the best content I found."

"Sounds like you found a lot of stuff trying to answer the *how*," I said. "Did you find anything exploring the *why*? Did you find anything on trying to answer these questions: Why do we have a cultural identity or why is cultural identity so important to humans?" Angel paused. "Not really," he said. "Most of the stuff I learned was really pragmatic. It wasn't trying to teach anything at a foundational level."

"Exactly!" I said. "So much of our cultural moment is about *how* to think and feel. It is about how to be your *authentic self*, but it does not talk about the why." I shared with Angel that the question we must answer before the *how* is, *Why* do we have a cultural identity? Only then can we move to the *how*. "The Scriptures help us answer *where* culture comes from and *why* we have a cultural identity!" I said to Angel. "Only then can we move to how to develop our identity. Meaning and purpose come before practice or action."

That conversation helped set Angel on a path to discern from the Scriptures what to think about his cultural identity. In the same way, this chapter will help us discern the where and why of cultural identity. This will be framed as a sacred identity outlook rooted in Scripture and Jesus.

Where does all culture come from?
Answer: From creator God.
Why do we have a cultural identity?
Answer: To display Jesus.
How do we reflect the image of Jesus in the world?
Answer: From our cultural location.

CONFORMED TO CHRIST

In the book of Romans, the apostle Paul teaches us something remarkable about the Christian life. Paul was writing to a culturally diverse group of Christians in the city of Rome. He says, "For those whom [God] foreknew he also predestined to be conformed to the image of his Son" (Romans 8:29). God knew about us before we were born. God knew our names. He knew what culture we were going to be born into. He knew our stories. God knew our faces. God knew we would be reading this book. God knew we would be following his Son. This is what *foreknew* means.

In the second part of the verse, we learn that God created us to be more like Jesus in the world. This is what it means *to be conformed to the image of his Son*. Those following Jesus must conform their lives to the person of Jesus. This verse has massive implications for our understanding of cultural identity. Paul is teaching a diverse cultural group of Christians that regardless of their ethnic background, everyone is meant to emulate Christ daily. Those from a Jewish background were to find ways to be like Jesus within their cultural identity. Likewise, Gentiles were meant to live and act like Jesus from within their own culture.

In this verse we learn that the very goal of our cultural identity can only be found in Jesus. The aim of our cultural identity is in Jesus. While this truth is something found in Scripture, broader Western culture teaches that your cultural identity is about you. Culture is about what you think and feel. Your identity is fixed in your own truth. Cultural identity is developed on your own terms.

DEFINING CULTURAL IDENTITY

Before we further contrast a sacred and secular view on cultural identity, let's define some terms.[1] Cultural identity can be understood as *the stories, values, or expressions that best define you*.[2] Cultural identity is the parts of who you are that are most important to you. Aspects of cultural identity include, but are not limited to, language, family, ethnicity, race, class, nationality, politics, sex and gender, age, and work.[3]

Language

Language refers to the use of words through verbal, written, or signed communication. Some assert that language is the cornerstone of all cultural expression.

Family

Family refers to the biologically connected individuals who instill morals and norms within an individual. We are socialized within our family to speak a certain language, eat specific food, and behave a certain way.

Ethnicity

Ethnicity refers to a group of people who share a common heritage that originates in a particular place of the world. It is often linked by ancestral origins that create a set of traditions or values.

Race

Race is a tool of social hierarchy that divides humans based on physical characteristics like skin color. Despite being a social construct rather than something rooted in biology, it continues to influence many aspects of life, including access to opportunities and how people are treated.

Class

Class refers to how much money you make, your education level, or what community you have access to live within. Class affects our cultural identity through our admittance to a certain lifestyle, opportunities, and even life expectancy.

Nationality

Nationality usually pertains to someone's loyalty and membership in a broader government organization. It often signifies a shared history, geographical boundaries, and political structures.

Politics

Political identity is often set within the nation you call home. Political identity is shaped by one's view of the public good, party affiliations, and attitudes toward governance.

Sex and gender

Sex and gender relate to how individuals understand themselves in relation to their biology, body, and gender-based social expectations. Sex and gender play a significant role in shaping a person's behavior, appearance, and societal roles.

Age

Age-based identity refers to the roles, capabilities, and values someone has based on their stage of life. Being part of a specific generation can also shape the collective values of people who are formed in a particular moment of history.

Work

Our work or professional role deeply shapes our identity as humans. Career heavily influences one's self-worth, social status, and financial mobility.

Which of these ten aspects most informs your own cultural identity? Which are central to your cultural identity? Perhaps it is your ethnic background, your family, or your nationality. You will notice that some of these identity markers can change. For example, your work or political identity might change over the course of your life. This means your cultural identity can evolve over time. Some of these aspects are fixed by birth. For example, your biological family, ethnicity, or age is not something you can control.[4]

TWO VIEWS ON CULTURAL IDENTITY

The formation of cultural identity can be traced to two primary starting points: secular or sacred.[5]

The secular outlook on cultural identity is rooted in self. The aim of this loop is to express yourself in the world. This view claims that a person is born into an identity shaped by evolutionary progress (biology) and social expectation (society). In this outlook, there is no room for God or spirituality.

This view is captive to the shifting desires of the individual, social expectation, and our biological tendencies. The secular loop does not integrate into a higher purpose but rather is lost to whatever expressions the individual desires. It is therefore fragmented and incomplete.

The sacred outlook on cultural identity is rooted in the doctrine of the *imago Dei* (Latin for "image of God"). The aim of this loop is to image Christ in the world. While rooted in the reality that we are spiritual creatures, this view also integrates our social and biological identity. Instead of looping into self, which shifts and changes over time, we integrate our cultural identity into the unchanging image of God. Once we do this, we are free to express our cultural identity in the world. This is the freedom we have in Christ! In the sacred culture loop, we are enlightened by our creator God to image Jesus from the cultural location in which we were born. Unlike the fragmentation of the secular loop, our identity is integrated and enlightened.

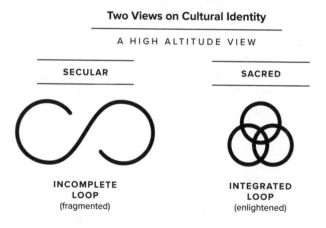

Two Views on Cultural Identity

A HIGH ALTITUDE VIEW

SECULAR

SACRED

INCOMPLETE
LOOP
(fragmented)

INTEGRATED
LOOP
(enlightened)

Secular cultural identity

Let's take a closer look at these two identity loops. The concept of *secularism* calls us to imagine culture and human identity without God. René Descartes, an Enlightenment philosopher, created a framework that pushed those in the West to think about cultural identity from the natural world, without God, when he famously said, "I think, therefore I am." This statement has framed much of the identity discovery process in the Western world in the centuries since.

In the secular cultural identity loop, the individual is the center. *Imago sui* is a Latin phrase that means "image of self." In the secular outlook, all ten aspects of cultural identity can be discovered or changed from within. Each category can be changed or moved based on the subjective thoughts, convictions, and feelings of an individual as they navigate the world around them.

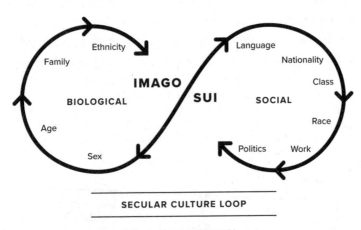

SECULAR CULTURE LOOP

Goal → Image self in world
Path → Cultural discovery through self
Results → Fragmented, Incomplete, Captive

In this loop, the projection of self is the map by which one navigates cultural identity. It is primarily about you. Imago sui upholds self-expression and self-reflection as the core values of cultural identity. Biology (nature) and society (nurture) serve the individual in the quest for the authentic self. On one side of the loop is *biology*. This represents the natural world and is marked by family, ethnicity, sex, and age (gender may also appear on the social side, as different cultures may have different expectations around sex and gender). On the other are *social* attributes. These aspects of cultural identity are shaped by the ever-changing movements of society—a person's work, nationality, class, politics, and so on can change, and one's identity with it.

In this outlook, whatever you think is true about your cultural identity becomes your *true* identity. Simply put, this view is about self-expression and self-discovery. A person finds their authentic self by navigating their view of body and society and then deciding what is right. If a person has spiritual beliefs, these views merely loop back into the self-discovery process. The secular culture loop ultimately leads to a captivity to self and society. Whereas popular culture positions this loop as freedom and liberty, as Christians we know there is no freedom without divine purpose and no liberty without Jesus.

Sacred cultural identity

Scripture provides a different perspective on cultural identity development. A sacred cultural identity places the individual in the context of a grand story. This story says that all humans have been made in the good image of God to reflect Christ in the world. We are free to image Christ in the world by integrating the ten aspects of cultural identity into God's purposes. In this view, we are called to integrate our biology (nature) and social expectations (nurture) into the Way of Jesus.

Imago Dei is at the center of the sacred identity loop. In the sacred outlook, God has granted each person a unique and beautiful cultural identity so they can reflect God in the world. God is the one who created the person and has given them a cultural identity. As in the secular loop, the individual navigates their biology (nature) and society (nurture). But when we understand our identity as sacred, we navigate these aspects of personhood in the context of Scripture, the spiritual rootedness of the body, and the gospel of Jesus. God has rooted our identity in the natural world and in society for the purpose of worshiping God. The follower of Jesus seeks to display the image of Christ in the world by asking, "How do I develop a cultural identity that honors and worships Jesus?"

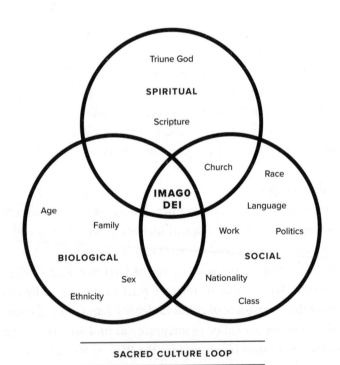

SACRED CULTURE LOOP

Goal → Image Christ in world
Path → Cultural discovery through Christ
Results → Enlightened, Integrated, Free

The concepts of cultural freedom and personal liberation are enclosed in the truth that our authentic self is found in Christ. It is not "I think, therefore I am" but rather "I'm created in God's good image, therefore I am!"

Is it easy for Christians to know how to integrate their biology and society into their cultural identity? No, it is still very hard—the natural world has been corrupted by sin. This means our biology and psychology have been corrupted. Our bodies decay, our families break, and we judge each other based on our ethnic heritage. This taints how we view ourselves and others. Likewise, the society in which we discover our identity has been built on corruption and injustice. The impacts of spiritual death on the world around us can make it difficult to navigate the biological and the social and integrate them into our spiritual identity.

When the secular loop asks, "How do I express my cultural identity in the world based on biology and society?," the answer is shaped by the individual. When the sacred loop asks, "How do I reflect the very good image of God based on nature and society?," the answer is shaped by the Way of Jesus.

The cultural identity loops can help us think about how the various parts of our identity interact and shape who we are. How have your morals and convictions been shaped by aspects of your cultural identity? Have parts of your culture changed over time? In what order of importance would you put each of these identity markers? Now consider how you are trying to conform your cultural identity to the image of God in the world. How does the Way of Jesus inform your view of self? How do the spiritual realities of God's world influence your view of your body and your cultural upbringing? For Christians, culture is what humans make of God's good creation!

3

JESUS, OUR KEY TO CULTURAL IDENTITY

Main point

▶ Jesus is the lens through which we understand all of Scripture.

In the first two chapters, we focused on how our cultural identity is sacred and can only be constructed in Christ. The aim of all human identity is not found in the self but in our creator Jesus.

Before we dive into our biblical survey, we need to establish a method by which to read the Scriptures. One way we can resist the urge to read in a culturally biased way is to understand the Bible on its own terms. So many problems have arisen because we fail to read the Bible properly. Conversely, when we read the Scriptures properly, we will unlock the purpose and meaning of our cultural identity.

The book of Hebrews points to Jesus as the arc and aim of Scripture. Hebrews was written to followers of Jesus to emphasize the superiority of Jesus Christ. The book is full of Old Testament heroes, Jewish practices, and appeals that

Jesus has satisfied the sacrificial system. It portrays Jesus as the ultimate high priest and the creator of all things. The book argues that regardless of a person's cultural background or upbringing, enlightenment is found in Christ alone.

> Long ago God spoke to our ancestors in many and various ways by the prophets, but in these last days he has spoken to us by a Son, whom he appointed heir of all things, through whom he also created the worlds. He is the reflection of God's glory and the exact imprint of God's very being, and he sustains all things by his powerful word. (Hebrews 1:1–3)

These beautiful verses point to the method by which we understand the Scriptures. While the Old Testament spoke to us "in many and various ways," God has spoken through Jesus in these "last days." God revealed the way that humans ought to live with Christ, the "exact imprint of God" on earth. Jesus, the stamp of God on earth, reveals God's will and desires for all humans. The implications of these verses are massive.

> In Jesus Christ, God has . . .
> sustained all human culture.
> shown us cultural enlightenment.
> provided a blueprint for humanity.

This means that as we read Scripture, we must keep the arc of God's story in mind. We must keep the Way of Jesus in mind. And we must consider how Jesus clarifies the ethics of the Old Testament. Why? We have been given the exact imprint of God's very being (v. 3)! Hebrews 1:1–3 helps frame our Bible study method throughout this entire book. To help us along the way, many of the chapters conclude with takeaways on how to read the Scriptures in light of the Way of Jesus.

BIBLE STUDY GONE WRONG

I must admit that I didn't always read the Bible this way. While growing up in church and attending Bible college, I was taught many other ways of studying the Bible. One study method in particular was burned into my mind from a young age. Before we tease out the implications of a Jesus-driven study method, let me share this other way with you to illustrate how *not* to read Scripture.

The year was 1997. I was eleven years old. At the preteen Sunday school class I regularly attended while my parents were in the main church service, the volunteer leaders tried hard to connect the Bible to the lives of us kids. They were good at it! On one particular Sunday, not many kids had shown up, so I was paired with an eighteen-year-old leader who was about to graduate from high school. His name was Adam. Instead of discussing the passage, Adam opened up to me about how hard it was for him to decide whether to get a full-time job or go to college. He was anxious about the decision. I felt bad for him. Thinking back on this moment, I recognize now that he was trying to turn his situation into a lesson for me. Adam looked at me, picked up his huge Bible, and said, "Sometimes when I don't know what to do, I close my eyes in prayer. Then I flip through my Bible and just stick my hand down onto a page. Then I open my eyes and read the first verse that I see. I take that verse to help decide what to do in life. This is how God speaks to us." Then, in an awkward twist, Adam put into practice what he just said. He closed his eyes, started flipping through the Bible, stopped somewhere late in the Old Testament, and stuck his finger down. I watched as he quietly read a verse from Ecclesiastes to himself. He turned to me with a smile and said, "God says I should go to college!" I smiled with him in an strange celebratory moment. I didn't learn until much later that this way to read the Bible isn't exactly normal. Looking back, I'm glad his finger didn't land on a passage about destroying the inhabitants of a city instead.

This story brings up a few important questions: How should we read the Bible? How do we know whether Adam was right or wrong in his approach? Without having a good answer to these questions, we are bound to turn the Bible into something it is not. Those with power will turn the Scriptures into a tool of oppression and violence. Those without power will turn the Bible into a tool to overthrow those in charge. Those with brazen personalities will justify harsh forms of communicating. Or people like Adam will develop a wacky approach to making important life decisions.

Everyone who reads the Bible imports their own experiences and cultural background into the text.[1] Yet if we only understand Scripture through our own cultural lenses, we end up blind to our biases and prejudices, and each cultural group will draw different interpretations.[2] It is critical to read and interpret the Scriptures the way the Bible tells us to. And the Scriptures teach us that Jesus enlightens the biblical text and sets us free from our own cultural blind spots.

SCRIPTURE UNLOCKED BY JESUS

We must begin by understanding that all of Scripture is pointing to the person of Jesus Christ.[3] The Scriptures tell us that Jesus is the ultimate key who unlocks the purpose of the Scriptures! To dig into this, we go to Luke 24 for a story that takes place on the road to Emmaus.

The story begins with Christ walking with two of Jesus' followers, who do not recognize him. It is shortly after Jesus'

crucifixion. While walking with the two people, Jesus inquires about their conversation. They share their disappointment that Jesus has been crucified—and now his body is missing from the tomb. They also mention that some women have reported that Jesus is alive. As they continue walking, Jesus tells the two men that the prophets had predicted this would happen. And then Jesus does something remarkable, positioning himself as the interpretive center of the Bible: "Beginning with Moses and all the prophets, he interpreted to them the things about himself in all the scriptures" (Luke 24:27).

In this verse, Jesus gives us the blueprint for understanding Scripture. Jesus teaches these two men how every Jewish prophet, both major and minor, points to Jesus. He makes clear that the stories, lessons, and characters from the Old Testament find their meaning in him. That the more than sixteen recorded prophets who spoke on behalf of God were all pointing to a fulfillment found in him. Indeed, all Scripture ultimately points to and testifies about his work (John 5:39). The thread pulling everything together is the person and work of Christ.[4]

The rest of the New Testament continues to point to Jesus as the person who unlocks our Bible. Later in Luke 24, Jesus says that everything has been fulfilled by him in the Law, Prophets, and Psalms (vv. 44–45). In the gospel of John, Philip teaches Nathanael that Moses points toward Jesus in the Law (John 1:45). Paul sits for an entire day convincing his listeners that the Law of Moses and the Prophets point to Christ (Acts 28:23). These are all critical examples that frame the way we read Scripture.[5]

With this in mind, we must read each Old and New Testament passage looking for Jesus. As we move through upcoming chapters, we will continue to ask the following questions: How is Jesus the key to this passage? How does Jesus clarify and give color to this text? How is this Old Testament passage pointing to the Way of Jesus? From Genesis all the way to Revelation, the Bible points to Jesus, finds its purpose in Jesus, and is pulling us to Christ.[6]

SCRIPTURE LEADING TO THE GOSPEL OF JESUS

There are two massive implications when we center Jesus as the hermeneutical key: Christ unlocks our understanding of the gospel and points us to true ethics.

The word *gospel* literally means "the good news"—Scripture specifically points to the good news that Jesus gave the world through his death and resurrection. When surveying the Bible, we quickly discover that the good news of Jesus is a response to problems in God's world. Humans rebel against God. Violence fills the world. Sinfulness corrupts culture. Israel engages in false worship, and the nations turn their backs on the Creator. Animals and the land are pillaged through war and conquest. What all this means is that we are less than God intended. The world is longing for a Savior. On the surface, this does not seem like good news. Yet the entire Bible is pointing to Jesus as the solution to the pain and desperation we feel in the world. For all the evil and hard moments in Scripture, we find good news in Jesus!

In Acts, Philip says that Jesus is the good news promised in Scripture. Acts 8:35 says, "Then Philip began to speak, and starting with this scripture he proclaimed to him the good news about Jesus." Luke the author of Acts is showing us that the Old Testament is pulling us toward the good news we have in Christ. Paul writes in 1 Corinthians 15:3–4, "For I handed on to you as of first importance what I in turn had received: that Christ died for our sins in accordance with the scriptures and that he was buried and that he was raised on the third day in accordance with the scriptures." From these verses we see again that the Bible is leading us to the good news found in Christ.

Who addresses the problem of evil? Jesus
Who brings good news into the world? Jesus.

Christ lived for us.
Christ died for us.
Christ resurrected for us.

The world is reborn—
identities reformed.
Roads leading home—
Christ, our beauty eternal.

Humans access the love of God by admitting that we need healing, allowing Jesus to be the center of our lives. This good news is an eternal light for our bodies and stories, and it has massive implications for cultural identity development. First, the goodness we long for in our cultural identity is only found in Jesus. He is the foundation and cornerstone by which we discover who we are; we can't find our cultural essence in any other place. Second, the cultural liberation we long for is found in Jesus. Our cultural identity only grows in Christ. The freedom we long for is found in following Jesus.[7]

SCRIPTURE POINTING TO THE WAY OF JESUS

Scripture is also clarified by the ethics that Jesus presents in the new covenant. Before churches had catchy names, the earliest groups of Christians were known simply as the Way. "The Way" is shorthand for the Way of Jesus. The book of Acts describes the earliest Christians

following the Way. In Acts 24:14, Paul says, "But this I admit to you, that according to the Way, which they call a sect, I worship the God of our ancestors, believing everything laid down according to the law or written in the prophets."

The Way informs our thinking.
The Way is how we talk and act.
The Way is how Christians live their lives.
The Way helps us navigate our feelings and culture.
The Way places Jesus Christ at the center of our
cultural identity.

The Scriptures teach that God fully revealed the Way of living in Jesus. Paul writes in Galatians 3:24 (NIV), "The law was our guardian until Christ came that we might be justified by faith." In other words, the hundreds of rules in the Mosaic law—always meant to help people manifest the imago Dei— find their fulfillment in Jesus. In Jesus, the ethics of God are clarified. In Christ, the salvation of God is revealed. This is the Way. Paul further emphasizes this in Colossians 2:9 (EHV): "The fullness of God's being dwells bodily in Christ." Jesus, the fullness of God, has shown us how humans ought to live in the world. John argues in his gospel that Jesus makes God known (John 1:18), that the Father and Son are one (10:30), and that Jesus came to reveal the Way on behalf of God the Father (14:10). This is further emphasized by Jesus himself when he claims to fulfill the Law and offer a more enlightened way of living in the world (Matthew 5:17–18). When Jesus says in the Sermon on the Mount in Matthew 5, "You have heard it said, . . . but I say to you . . . " he is contrasting the Old Testament Law with moral teachings known as the Way. Jesus fulfills the Law from the Old Testament in order to usher in a new way of living.

While reading the Bible, we must reflect on each passage in light of the teachings of Jesus. When we come across passages that conflict with Jesus' teachings, we must defer to what Jesus says in order that we remain conformed to the image of Christ (Romans 8:29). This is the Way!

What does God look like on earth? Jesus.
What does the will of God look like in action? Jesus.
Where can we find the good news from God? The Way of Jesus.
What ethical standard are the Scriptures pointing toward? The Way.
Where is each book and prophet pointing toward? The gospel of Jesus.
Who dignifies and clarifies our cultural identity?
We find this in Jesus—the one who shows us the Way.

For those reading Scripture, this means that Jesus clarifies how humans are to act in the world. Our ethics and morals are to be rooted in Jesus. Regardless of your cultural identity or where you fall on the cultural spectrum, you are bound to follow the Way.

When reading the Bible and navigating our cultural location, we must imagine ourselves walking alongside Jesus. We, like those walking with Jesus on the road to Emmaus, must place our trust in Christ. We must listen to how Jesus lived. We must read the Old Testament while considering the good news of Jesus. We must look for cultural clarity as we walk behind the One who created us in his good image.[8]

TAKEAWAYS

We should read the Scriptures through the lens of the gospel.

All the scriptures, from Old Testament to New Testament, are pointing toward the good news of Jesus. For those following the Way, we should be reading the Old Testament stories while considering where the story is headed. All the violence, destruction, broken families, destroyed creation, false worship, and devastated cultures should be understood with God's ultimate intention in Christ. We must keep what God has done in Christ at the forefront—especially as we consider the topic of cultural identity.

Jesus Christ is the ethical center of Scripture.

While there are many lessons to be learned in the Old Testament, the moral core of the text is found in Jesus. God sent Jesus to clarify how humans are to live, act, speak, and manifest the imago Dei in the world. We will find big tensions between how God called Israel to relate to the cultural other and what Jesus teaches us. In these cases, we keep the ethics of Jesus in mind while reading the Old Testament. We defer to the ethics of Jesus. We remember that while Israel represented God to the nations, the gospel of John tells us that Jesus is the perfect representation of God on earth.

Individuals are to express the Way from their cultural location.

In the same way that Jesus is the key to the Scriptures, Jesus is the key to our cultural identities. In the following chapters, our biblical survey will help us see how Jesus desires that we manifest the Way of Jesus from our own unique cultural perspectives. Regardless of your unique cultural narrative or how you construct your culture loop, God has called you to follow Jesus. It is important to consider how best to do this in how God has already created you.

Part II

OLD TESTAMENT AND CULTURE

4

THE IMAGO DEI

Genesis 1:26–28

Main point

▶ Jesus dignifies human culture by creating
all people in the image of God.

Genesis is the origin story that undergirds all cultural narratives.[1] The book of Genesis is meant to give identity
and purpose to every tribe, tongue, and nation. In a world of
competing values and stories, this ancient text helps us understand who we are and how to frame our cultural identity.

RUKUNDO'S WORDS
I first want to highlight a cross-cultural friendship that helped
me see the teaching of the imago Dei more clearly. In 2007, I
had the privilege of teaching Bible classes at Africa Renewal
University just north of Kampala, Uganda. During my time
there, I interacted with students from all over Eastern and
Central Africa. Fresh out of Bible college, I was looking to
better understand the global church and learn about African
cultures. During one of my first classes, I met a student named

Rukundo Rodger. We became fast friends. Rukundo was living in Uganda to receive pastoral training before returning to his home country of Rwanda. I learned that his mother had become a refugee to Uganda around the start of the 1994 Rwandan genocide. While sitting over lunch, he explained that his mom had then returned to their home country to fight for the Rwandan Patriotic Front while he was left back in Uganda as a child. This army eventually liberated Rwanda from the Hutus in the aftermath of the hundred-day genocide, during which one million Tutsis were tortured and killed by their fellow Hutu countrypeople. Rukundo was of Tutsi descent.

I had the opportunity to visit Rwanda, and I was taken aback by the beauty of the people, the rolling green hills, and the richness of the culture. When I walked the countryside with Rukundo, the sun always seemed to keep us at the perfect temperature. I was also able to visit the churches and hospitals where thousands of Tutsis had been killed during the genocide. Rukundo said to me, "Even though those in power thought it just to kill my people, it was evil because we have all been made in the image of God. Each one of us has eternal worth and value, even though we come from different tribes and speak different languages." Rukundo's words stuck with me.

In this chapter we will explore the very doctrine that Rukundo cited in our conversation. It is a teaching called the imago Dei. This truth, rooted in the book of Genesis, was central to Rukundo's belief that although his people were a marginalized cultural group, they, like each and every one of us, have been given a value worth protecting.

JESUS AND THE IMAGO DEI

In the very first chapter of Genesis, we learn that God created the heavens and earth, light and darkness, land and sea, day and night, plants and trees, sea creatures and birds. These created pairings took place from days one through five of creation. God created, creation burst forth, and it was good. Then, something remarkable happened on day six.

> Then God said, "Let us make humans in our image, according to our likeness." (Genesis 1:26)

God decided to make humans in the image of God. In Latin, the phrase, "the image of God" is translated as the *imago Dei*.[2] God uniquely made humans to reflect the divine image in the world. God did not make the land in his image. God didn't make the moon and stars in his image. God didn't make the ocean, birds, or other mammals in his image. Yahweh made the intentional decision to create you, me, all people who have ever lived, in his image.

When these verses were written, the nations surrounding Israel were creating golden figures and statues to represent gods in the world. God guides Israel in a different direction by saying, "You . . . my people . . . are my image in the world." Israel did not need to commission an artist to create an image of God, because they were the image of God in the world! Yahweh followers aren't supposed to create these kinds of idols because humanity already *is* the image of God. God's design is that humanity itself would represent the Creator in the world.

Cultural expression

There are three central teachings from Genesis 1:26 that shape how we think about our cultural identity. The first is that humans image God through their unique cultural identities. Genesis teaches that God created Adam and Eve fixed to a time, place, land, and language. In other words, God created the first humans as embodied cultural creatures. The creator God binds each of us to a cultural location. When you eat your favorite food, you image God. When you speak your mother language, you image God in the world. When you get together with family, you bear God's image. When telling a joke or singing a song, you spread the colorful image of God in the room. When you cry after a hard day, you image the divine.

Beyond cultural expressions, even our bodies are a manifestation of the imago Dei. Your skin color, hair type, facial structure, sex, and height image God. The yet-to-be-born, newly born, children, teens, middle-aged, elderly, and those on their deathbed all image our creator God. God inescapably shines through us like the sun shining through the atmosphere to the surface of the earth. You and I bear the mark of the divine in how we express our culture in the world.

Cultural community

The second teaching from Genesis 1:26 is that humans were created to display God's divine mark in the context of community. Even before humans were created, God fashioned a world set within a solar system that is fully reliant on its sun. God then made land, seas, animals, trees, and a delicate ecosystem to sustain life. After which, we humans were created to be fully dependent on our surroundings. God created humans to form cultural identity from within the community of creation—not outside of it. God sets us free in the interplay of the animals, the land, our human counterparts, and our creator God. We find our own identity in the context of those around us. Our family. Our friends. The ones we love and who love us.

Genesis teaches us that without our connections to land, animals, and our Creator, cultural identity does not exist. We discover who we are in the context of our physical location and within the very spaces in which we have grown up. The cultural community found in Genesis stands in stark contrast to the Western way of understanding identity. The Western world says you have the power to self-determine your identity. The Scriptures teach that we have a community-determined identity. We are first known in community with God, others, and the rest of creation.

Cultural dignity

Finally, God endowed all image bearers with cultural dignity. Every person has irrevocable worth before God. This inherent cultural dignity means that it is wrong to consider one cultural identity superior to another. These kinds of judgments are typically shaped by the many cultural preferences fostered by the places where we grew up. But these differences have been developed over tens of thousands of years by humans made in God's image, each reflecting God in unique and important ways. While we tend to judge others who do not hold our cultural outlook, God has made all in God's image to live, work, and build family community without judging others.

Some people groups are very individualistic. Some live more collectively. Some are direct communicators whereas others passively make their point. Some people value timeliness and scheduling their lives. Others are event-driven and will allow community to dictate their day. Many people express their faith through order and quiet. Others express themselves through the beautiful noises of song and dance. Some gather around foods filled with spices and aromatics whereas other cultural palates lean toward savory and sweet flavors. Some dress up by wearing less while others dress up by wearing more clothes. The list goes on! Instead of judging people based on these differences, we should be finding God's good image in those who are different from us!

If God dignifies all humans as made in God's image, then it follows that Jesus dignifies our cultural differences. When humans rob others of their ability to express themselves within these categories, we fail to reflect God in the world. While the Bible does speak about right and wrong, it does not comment on the thousands of cultural preferences that humans hold. These extrabiblical cultural preferences should be dignified equally. If humans equally image God in the abundance of our cultural habits, then we must create space for our fellow humans to embody those preferences.

The Rwandan genocide is an example of the judgment we often make toward those who do not inhabit our own cultural identity. When taken to an extreme, we act out violently toward those holding different cultural outlooks, leading to hate speech, bullying, public shaming, violence, war, and even genocide. History is full of examples of human failure to dignify the cultural other in keeping with the imago Dei.

CULTIVATION IN GOD'S WORLD

Let's continue on in the Genesis 1 story:

> Then God said, "Let us make humans in our image, according to our likeness, and let them have dominion over the fish of the sea and over the birds of the air and over the cattle and over all the wild animals of the earth and over every creeping thing that creeps upon the earth."
> So God created humans in his image,
>   in the image of God he created them;
>   male and female he created them.
> God blessed them, and God said to them, "Be fruitful and multiply and fill the earth and subdue it." (vv. 26–28)

Humans, we read, were meant to have dominion over creation. *Dominion* means to spread into the world, cultivate the land, and care for creation. This doesn't mean we have a mandate to do whatever we want with the earth; humans are to reflect the imago Dei by becoming caretakers and stewards of the earth, of all creation. God connects us to nature, including the land and the animals. The dominion that God gives humans is a great responsibility we hold. Regardless of our cultural location, we must care for animals, move through the world in a hospitable spirit, and engage the land with respect.

Foundational aspects of cultural identity: Body, sex and gender, and family

These verses reveal three important developments in cultural identity—body, sex and gender, and family. The cultural intersections of body, sex and gender, and family are inescapable across all cultures.

Genesis presents the complex truth that you can understand your cultural identity only in relationship to your human body and your family of origin. The intersections of body, sex, and family are presented in Genesis as foundational pieces to our cultural identity. These cultural intersections are sacred. They are also complex. Since sin affects all creation, our sexuality and our gender identity and our family of origin can also be painful or confusing aspects of our identity.

There are some important truths we must understand about these intersections. First, all people are made with equal dignity and worth. In most periods of world history, men have sought to dominate women. Even in recent history we have seen massive wage gaps between men and women, unequal voting rights, and educational opportunities denied based on unjust gender norms. The gender disparities manifested across cultures show that we have not taken this passage seriously. Where many cultures treat women as lesser than men, Genesis teaches us that all humans bear God's mark equally.

Second, men have historically weaponized the command to take dominion to ransack creation and dehumanize others, especially women. When considering these verses, we must be careful to avoid interpretations that justify violence toward vulnerable bodies and cultural groups as well as toward nature itself.

Third, the body was created as a sacred expression of God's image. Where the Western world teaches us to use the body for the purposes of work and pleasure, Genesis presents something better. Our bodies are for community, for sacred work, for human relationships, and for caring for the created world. While we can also use our bodies for work and pleasure, in the West we have tended to lean too deeply into these impulses and not enough into the fuller vision of what our bodies are for. We need a more embodied and peaceful approach to what it means to bear God's image in the world.

Finally, we learn that humans cultivate their identity within the context of their family unit. Though families can take many forms, everyone was brought into this world through a biological mother and father. Our family units can be a painful reality for some who have been harmed by loved ones. Others embrace their family unit as a place of personal joy and freedom.

Whether there is positive, negative, or mixed experience with our family and our sexuality and gender, these aspects have a massive impact on our cultural identity development. The degree to which someone is supposed to embrace their body, sex and gender, and family identity is debated among

Bible interpreters. While this book does not focus on resolving those tensions, which have many complications and nuances, it is critical to consider the biological reality of the bodies that God gives us. For example, if we are supposed to form our identity in the context of the material world that God created, then we must consider how our gendered body fits into that identity. If the land, sun, moon, dirt, and physical location matter to our cultural identity, then our gendered bodies matter as well. At the same time, Christians must consider the harmful societal expectations around gender that damage our view of self and those who are different from us.

TAKEAWAYS

Human culture reflects the likeness of God.

Jesus created humans to manifest the likeness of God in the world. Every person reflects God in the culturally specific ways they think, act, and emote. Each human language expresses God. Every ethnic group naturally manifests the imago Dei. Each gender and class of people equally reflects God's image in the world. History reveals over and over that we devalue people based on race, age, immigration status, age, gender, and ethnicity. Genesis shows us a better way. We must treat all people, regardless of their cultural identity, as image bearers of God.

God dignifies our cultural differences.

There are sweeping differences in how humans live culturally. We handle conflict differently. We raise children, eat food, celebrate, create art, enter the workforce, and relate to time differently. The problem that most cultures face is that we take the preference of our culture and expect others to accommodate us. We translate strange as *wrong*. We consider different *sinful.* We push our cultural defaults on others by expecting those from other cultures to adapt to our way or get out of the way. Genesis 1 confronts this way of being in the world. This way of being contradicts the Way of Jesus. We can't manifest the image of God in the world if we carry a spirit of cultural elitism or domination over others.

5

THE TABLE
OF NATIONS

Genesis 10

Main point

▶ Humans reflect the imago Dei by filling
the world with cultural diversity.

A few years ago, my family moved to Tucson, Arizona. Tucson is marked by a hot, dry climate and a national park full of beautiful, mountainous topography. It was no surprise that we landed in the sunny desert, because my wife Sarswatie is Caribbean, and she needs the sun. She doesn't like the sun or think that sun is great—she *needs* it. Her favorite time of day is the evening, when the sun is setting behind our house. While sitting in the back of our house, we can see an array of colors that slowly move from bright to dim. When the sun nears the horizon, it seems as if the sky expands into a landscape painting. Orange mixes with yellow. Yellow touches red. Then the colors dance away while blue and black slowly overcome the sky. The colors of sunset are then replaced by the light from the moon and thousands of stars slowly appearing with a 360-degree view. It is stunning.

Scientists note that while the sun consistently projects the same light to earth, it can produce many different colors—blue, green, cyan, orange, red, yellow, and violet. These colors often mix to produce dozens of shades that we can pick up with our eyes. Even though the sun shines yellow, it produces hundreds of other colors as it floods through the earth's atmosphere.

In the same way the sun creates different colors through our atmosphere, Jesus as the Word has intentionally created different cultures throughout the world. Though we have one Creator, there are many cultural colors in our world. Humans have the privilege of embodying one of God's many cultural shades. The colors of culture we all inhabit were created intentionally by God to be good. From our mother language to our skin color, from our nation of origin to our hair type, God desired the world to be diverse from the beginning. How do we know this to be true? Genesis 10 reveals to us that God desires the various colors to emit the imago Dei across the world.

GOD DESIGNED DIVERSITY

Over the next few chapters, we will explore how, from the beginning of world history, God created humans to spread into the world as a cultural mosaic. God intended diversity. God designed the world to be filled with thousands of cultural colors that reflect the imago Dei in an assortment of wonder. Is multiculturalism good? Does God want us to speak different languages and emit different cultural shades? In the book of Genesis, God answers these questions with a resounding *yes*.

A lot happens between Genesis 1 and Genesis 10. As we explored in the previous chapter, in Genesis 1:26–28, God creates humans in God's image to go into the world to create families, cultivate the world, and care for creation. But then Adam and Eve reject God's command in the garden and eat the forbidden fruit. This results in sin entering the human experience. Sin places distance between God and humans. Disharmony befalls the children of Adam and Eve. After leaving the garden of Eden, things only grow worse. After a worldwide flood, Noah's descendants are given a fresh chance to fulfill the commission given to Adam and Eve. Once again, God is telling his people to *go into the world.*

THE TABLE OF NATIONS

This leads us to Genesis 10—a chapter often called "The Table of Nations."[1] As we consider this chapter, let's pay attention to a few important questions: Did God want humans to have one universal culture with one language? Or did God want humans to manifest the imago Dei through many different cultural identities?

After the worldwide flood subsided (as described in the story of Noah), the various continents of the world emerged. The wooden ark that carried the family of Noah hit dry ground. In Genesis 9:1 we read, "God blessed Noah and his sons and said to them, "Be fruitful and multiply and fill the earth." You might notice that this is the exact command given to Adam and Eve earlier in Genesis 1:26–28.

Genesis 10 teaches that all people who came after Noah had a common origin story and joint ancestry rooted in this reestablishment of God's command. Moving from this common story, we see Noah's sons Shem, Ham, and Japheth moving their families into different locations across the ancient Near East.

Let's look at the progression from verses 1 through 32. The various aspects of cultural identity that the passage highlights are in italic.

Verse 1 These are the descendants of Noah's sons; . . . children were born to them after the flood.

Verse 2 The descendants of Japheth . . .

Verse 5 in their *lands*, with their own *language*, by their *families*, in their *nations*.

Verse 6 The descendants of Ham . . .

Verse 20 by their *families*, their *languages*; their *lands*, and their *nations*.

Verse 22 The descendants of Shem . . .

Verse 31 by their *families*, their *languages*, their *lands*, and their *nations*.

Verse 32 These are the families of Noah's sons, according to their genealogies, in their *nations* . . .

In this passage, we see four aspects of culture emerge: land, language, family, and nation. These verses highlight the intentions of God's command to Adam and Eve to go into the world: The families of Japheth, Ham, and Shem travel on dry land to express the imago Dei by inhabiting different cultural identities. They speak different languages, create different kinship circles, and forge different nations. This diversity was blessed (Genesis 9:1) and envisioned by God from the beginning.

Let us take a closer look at these four aspects highlighted in Genesis 10:

Land

The first aspect of cultural identity highlighted in verses 5, 20, and 31 is land. The Hebrew word for "land" can also be understood to represent country, territory, region, or geographical location. Genesis 10 shows that God desired these early travelers to spread into the world to inhabit different geographical regions. The land became a natural barrier or passage for economic, military, or political movements. The land also became a central marker for who they were as a people.

Land and location have a deep effect on our cultural identity. Think about the various foods we eat, the ways we create our dwellings, or the clothes we wear. This is largely shaped by the land and climate in which we live. We have different needs, challenges, and available materials. Over time, the descendants of Noah would inevitably have developed different cultural practices based on the land in which they lived. Those in the mountains became "mountain people," whereas those along water developed cultural practices as "water people." The land we live on is the land that we live with. If we stop working with and in the soil, we give up a central part of our cultural identity. Land and geography matter deeply to who we are as people.

Language

The second aspect of cultural identity highlighted in verses 5, 20, and 31 is language. The word for "language" in Hebrew can be translated as "tongues" or "speech." In Genesis 10 we learn that God sent out Noah's family to develop different languages. This meant the descendants of Noah developed various forms of communication that were unique to their people. This influenced not just how they spoke and what words they used, but also the art they created and how they processed information. The languages they developed also had a deep impact on how they passed down important information from one person to the next, from one generation to the next. As part of the fulfillment of God's command to fill the earth (9:1), the people of Japheth, Ham, and Shem all spoke different tongues.

Language can be understood as the cornerstone of all human culture. The written, spoken, or signed words we use daily are foundational to our communication across family, work, politics, and other parts of daily life. Language binds us together and segments us into distinct cultural groupings. Without question, one of the main reasons we have such distinct cultural identities across our world is the beautiful difference within languages.

Family

The third aspect of cultural identity highlighted in these verses is family. The word for "family" in Hebrew often translates as "tribe," "clan," "kindred," or "people." Genesis 10 defines family as those who are closest to you—those living together as your smallest, most core grouping of people. Family is the people with whom we grow up and share a dwelling. The people who live around us, who take care of us, those we are obligated to take care of. In the ancient Near East, families were often marked by biological grandparents, parents, aunts and uncles, cousins, and siblings.

In that time, people lived in local communities that were not connected by modern travel or technology. Family, clan, and tribe were interconnected cultural circles. When you put multiple families together, you created clans. When you put multiple clans together, you created tribes. These circles of family, clan, and tribe become a people dependent on one another for community and survival. This aspect of cultural identity was essential for communities to flourish.

Nation

The fourth aspect of cultural identity highlighted in these verses is nation. The Hebrew word for "nation" usually refers to one of the largest cultural groupings. A nation in the ancient Near East usually drew geographical boundaries, had a shared political system, spoke a unifying language, and held to a similar religion. Families, clans, and tribes often came together to create nations. Nations also sought to expand their power through warfare or defend their borders through defensive measures. Nations typically had a set of religious practices that were maintained and defended by the people from the capital city.

In Scripture, nations are one of the most common cultural groupings. God ends up creating the people of Israel. This Jewish nation, or people, established a kingdom (which later divided into kingdoms, plural) and existed among the surrounding nations of Egypt, Babylon, Assyria, and so on. These nations are major players in the biblical story. Throughout world history we see humans naturally create nations, big and small, to attempt to protect their people and govern their citizens with the best interest of their people in mind. At other points of history, nations have been created or used to oppress entire groups of people or maintain ethnic or tribal superiority within their region.

In this passage, we see that before God called a people, who became a nation with borders, the foundations of cultural identity are present. As professor of New Testament Steven M. Bryan writes in *Cultural Identity and the Purposes of God*, God's intention for humans to spread diversely into the world "tells us that God created human beings for, rather than with, cultural identity."[2] The cultures we are born into are not random but rather a beautiful example of God's design. It was the purpose of God for each of us to inhabit a specific cultural identity. This should lead us to ask: For what purpose did God bring me into this cultural location? How do I better reflect

God's image from my cultural perspective? We will carry these implications forward as we survey the rest of Scripture!

TAKEAWAYS

Jesus intends humans to express the imago Dei through cultural differences.

Diversity is God's desire! Jesus dignifies our differences—from the young to the old, from undocumented individuals to citizens, from refugees to those who are lifelong residents of the same place, from dark-skinned to light-skinned, from those speaking an obscure language to those speaking Spanish, from the quiet to the loud, from those who press into conflict to those who avoid it, from those living on the coast to those who are landlocked, from those with no education degrees to some with too many degrees. God loves the diversity that began unspooling in Genesis 10 and loves the cultural nuances of our lives today.

Humans naturally cluster with their people in specific locations.

Even amid diversity, we humans tend to group with our own people. We tend to remain within the cultural groups in which we were raised. Genesis 10 dignifies that instinct. It is okay to be with your people and remain in your cultural grouping. Yet while embracing our own cultural location, we can never lose sight of God's beauty in diversity. We must remain aware of the biases, prejudices, and blind spots of our own people and cultural identity. While it is normal to find refuge in our cultural norms, we must be ready to press beyond them.

The Way of Jesus should foster an appreciation for cultural differences.

If God desires that humans manifest the imago Dei in distinct and different cultural groups, we should humbly learn about the cultural other and find interest in different ways of life. Followers of Jesus should respectfully learn about the language, food, dress, and cultural expressions of those different from them. Do you find yourself curious to discover the imago Dei in those who hold a different cultural identity? As Jesus followers, we should embrace cultural differences, even if they make us uncomfortable, as manifestations of God's presence in those who did not grow up like us.

6

THE TOWER OF BABEL

Genesis 11:1–9

Main point

▶ Humanity chose cultural uniformity in place of God's plan for cultural diversity.

The very next story in Genesis is known as the Tower of Babel. We will read and interpret this story considering God's command to fill the earth (Genesis 1:26–28) and the way Noah's kids began to fulfill this command through cultural diversity (10:1–9). It is important to read the story of Babel in the context of these previous passages. The fact that the author of Genesis placed the Table of Nations right before the Tower of Babel story tells us something about God's design for diversity.

Genesis 11 begins:

Now the whole earth had one language and the same words. And as they migrated from the east, they came upon a plain in the land of Shinar and settled there. And they

said to one another, "Come, let us make bricks and fire
them thoroughly." And they had brick for stone, and bitu-
men for mortar. (vv. 1–3)

The story starts by mentioning that humanity had one language and migrated together to the land of Shinar. The land
of Shinar is also identified with Sumer, an ancient civilization
and historical region in southern Mesopotamia, which is modern-day Iraq. This was an arid desert land that would have
been a difficult place to settle. Burning bricks together meant
that the people were serious about making a settlement for
their people.

Then they said, "Come, let us build ourselves a city and a
tower with its top in the heavens, and let us make a name
for ourselves; otherwise we shall be scattered abroad upon
the face of the whole earth." (v. 4)

The people created an outpost for humanity where they
could stay together. This represents two areas of disobedience for these settlers. First, the people wanted to make a
name for themselves. This seems to indicate they wanted to
build a culture around their own power rather than God's.
They wanted to create a nation or ancient civilization in their
way. To "make a name for ourselves" meant that they focused
on what they could achieve without God. But throughout
Scripture, God constantly calls humans to build their life
and identity on God alone. The ancient story is a modern
warning for those who would build any part of their identity
outside of God.

Second, we learn that the people who settled in Shinar
refused to fulfill God's mandate in Genesis 1:26–28. In the
second part of verse 4, the people narrate, "Let us build

ourselves a city, otherwise we will be scattered abroad upon the face of the whole earth." They were resistant to God's command to spread into the world. The people did not want to go any farther. Perhaps they were afraid of the frontier. Perhaps they were comfortable in their unifying language and culture. They didn't see any reason to spread out, so they built a tower up. Whereas Noah's descendants began to fulfill the creation mandate through spreading diversely, those building a tower in Shinar intentionally stopped spreading and remained a culturally uniform people. This was in direct contrast to God's command, "Be fruitful and multiply. Fill the earth and subdue it" (1:28). How would God respond?

> The LORD came down to see the city and the tower, which mortals had built. And the LORD said, "Look, they are one people, and they have all one language; and this is only the beginning of what they will do; nothing that they propose to do will now be impossible for them. Come, let us go down and confuse their language there, so that they will not understand one another's speech." (11:5–7)

God came down and confused the languages of the people, creating many new languages. This made it difficult for the people to communicate. Yet verse 6 says that nothing would be impossible if the people continue creating a unified culture. This does not mean that humans can rival God or that humans can overpower God. It seems that God confused them because of their growing desire to create without relying on their Creator. God decided to teach them that there are real consequences for believing you can be great outside of God. Pride comes with a fall. Also, it seems clear from the narrative that God was not pleased with their rejection of the creation mandate of Genesis 1:26–28. When the people of Shinar refused to go into the world to create diverse communities, they chose homogeneity and uniformity over the divine desire for diversity.

Some Bible interpreters claim that because God punished Shinar by creating different languages, diversity is not God's design but a result of sin. This is not an honest reading of the text, for several reasons. It is critical to explore the punishment of God as a reinforcement of what the people were supposed to be doing all along! Imagine a twelve-year-old whose mother tells him to clean the guest room in their apartment. The son refuses to leave the living room while watching TV. The mom comes to her son, turns off the TV, hands him the cleaning supplies, and says, "Go clean the room right now. No more TV this weekend." In this case, the punishment for the son is forcing him to do what he was already supposed to do! In light of the whole story we've explored so far, God created more languages not as a random punishment, but to force the people to do what they were supposed to be doing all along.

Second, it's important that the author placed the story of the Table of Nations before Babel. If the Table of Nations came after Babel, then it could be argued that diversity is a result of sin. Yet we are told that Noah's descendants carried out the Genesis 1:26–28 / 9:1 mandate to fill the earth before Babel. Nowhere in the Tower of Babel story does God say that the creation of more languages is bad or evil. God seemed to punish the people of Shinar by forcing them to do what God intended from the beginning. And when we piece the rest of the Old Testament and New Testament together, we see that God's ultimate design in Jesus Christ is to gather a diverse people for worship of God. We don't see Jesus come to create one language, one nation, or one ethnic group—the arc of

Scripture shows us that the diversity coming out of the Table of Nations is the true call of humanity.[1]

Genesis 11 continues:

> So the LORD scattered them abroad from there over the face of all the earth, and they left off building the city. Therefore it was called Babel, because there the LORD confused the language of all the earth; and from there the LORD scattered them abroad over the face of all the earth. (vv. 8–9)

The passage ends with God forcing the people of Shinar to scatter and fill the earth. This was the loving push of a just God who does not tolerate human pride, insisting that they fulfill the Genesis 1:26–28 mandate to fill the world.

TAKEAWAYS

Cultural identity is established through God alone.

Those of us who grew up in the West are taught that we can create and foster our cultural identity outside of God. When considering our identity, the West teaches that God is optional. God can be a second or third thought when considering our ethnicity, our daily cultural habits, or our work. This passage teaches us that we do not start with *self* when considering our cultural identity; we must start with the one who created us. At Shinar, we learn about a people looking to develop their essence, their identity, and their work outside of God. Yet God commanded this ancient group of people to spread the imago Dei into the world.

The Way of Jesus calls us to new and faithful cultural frontiers.

The Tower of Babel is an ancient warning for those of us who fear cross-cultural engagement. It can be easy for us to settle in one cultural location—both literally and figuratively. Yet just like the call for the ancient peoples to go into unknown places for the sake of God's purposes, Jesus is calling us into the daily frontier of neighbor love and cultural humility. This is how we manifest the imago Dei and forge a better path than those building a comfortable tower. Instead of building a monocultural tower, Jesus calls us to set a culturally inclusive table.

7

BLESSED TO BE A CULTURAL BLESSING

Genesis 12:1–3

Main point

▶ God created Israel to bless all cultures of the earth.

The Tower of Babel story leaves us with a massive question: How will God reach the new peoples spread across the world? This brings us to Genesis 12! To rescue the world from sin, spiritual death, and social languishing, God decided to create a nation through the person Abram. Up until this point in the story, God didn't prefer a language, a specific people, a geographical location, or a nation. This all changes in Genesis 12.

Abram, who would later be known as Abraham, came from Mesopotamia. He was born in Ur of the Chaldeans, a region known for its trade routes and craftsmanship. This region was polytheist, which means most people worshiped multiple gods. The moon god Nanna was especially popular. As a member of this society, Abram would have been familiar with the cultural practices and beliefs prevalent in Ur.

In Genesis 12:1, God says to Abram,

> Go from your country and your kindred and your father's house to the land that I will show you.

God tells Abram to leave his home nation and his clan. Abram is directed to leave the circles of trust and the culturally safe spaces for a new land. Abram would be leaving behind an ancient urban center in Mesopotamia for a life of nomadic wandering in pursuit of something he did not yet understand. Abram would trade allegiance to many gods for belief in one God. He would trade cultural comfort for cultural insecurity. He is asked to step out in faith for a God who has not yet shown his power. Why is Abram being called to do this?

> I will make of you a great nation, and I will bless you and make your name great, so that you will be a blessing. (v. 2)

God tells Abram that he will create a great nation that will be blessed by God. God's blessing means that Abram and his children will be safe and protected, his family will have enough to eat, and his people will not suffer from war or famine. In that time, to be *blessed* was a sign that you had a deep connection to God. If you were blessed, the land would produce, and God would listen to your prayers. At the end of verse 2, Abram finds out that God's blessing will extend beyond his people. God says, "So that you will be a blessing." This is key in the covenant that God is establishing with Abram. God will bless Abram, create a nation, and make his name great so that all the peoples of the world will be blessed. God's intent is to safeguard all people, provide enough food for all people, and provide home for all people.

The nation that God would create through Abram was Israel. Israel was commissioned by God to spread spiritual, social, and cultural flourishing to the world. God went from calling all people to go into the world diversely to calling a specific nation and people to bless the world—a blessing meant to spill out over the millions of people who inhabited every cultural space across the world. From one culture, all would be blessed. From one nation, all would be loved. From one ethnic group, all nations would flourish.

We continue in Genesis 12:3:

> I will bless those who bless you, and the one who curses you I will curse, and in you all the families of the earth shall be blessed.

This scripture reveals the flip side of the agreement God is making with Abram. God will support the people who support Israel. God will care for them and create good things for those nations. Conversely, God will hurt and harm the nations that stand against the nation of Israel. While God promises to protect Israel, the ultimate intention of Yahweh—to cause good for every cultural group of the world—is made clear at the end of verse 3. Israel will be blessed, and through their abundant flourishing, the world will receive blessing.

OLD COVENANT ESTABLISHED

From this point forward, the Old Testament scriptures reveal God's desire to promote cultural flourishing through God's people. God desired that the whole world be saved through the cultural people of Israel. This Jewish cultural identity was marked by a mixture of social, political, ancient Near Eastern, and Mesopotamian practices. These cultural practices were filtered through the Hebrew language, through God's direct revelation to the prophets, and through hundreds of commands within the Mosaic law. God's chosen cultural identity would be marked by membership in the nation of Israel, worship of God in the city Jerusalem, and specific Jewish practices that created a unique cultural identity. To be an ethnic Jew was to be chosen by God.

The chart depicts cultural identity as reflected in the old covenant of the Old Testament and the new covenant of Jesus. The middle column reflects what cultural identity looked like for God's chosen people in the Old Testament. The final column is where we are headed as we survey the topic of cultural identity in the New Testament.

Cultural Identity across the Covenants

	Old covenant	New covenant
Leadership	Priests, prophets, and kings	King Jesus Christ
Nation	Israel	All nations
Location	Temple in Jerusalem	Temple in all people
Language	Hebrew	All languages
Expressions	Jewish identity Torah, circumcision, feasts, temple, sacrifice	Interethnic identity Faith, baptism, communion, etc.
Covenant faithfulness	Adopt a Jewish cultural identity	Convert who remains in native cultural identity

While reading through the middle column, do you feel the tension in this story development? I certainly feel a little uneasy when considering the impact on cultural identity. In creating Israel, God moved toward cultural exclusion. What did this tangibly mean? No matter where you were in the world, you were supposed to follow the Jewish patriarchs. Regardless of your ethnic identity, you needed to adopt ethnic practices of the Jews. Regardless of your urban dwelling, Jerusalem was the true holy city. Hebrew was the chosen language of God. Despite your unique cultural celebrations, you needed to follow the feasts and festivals set out by God in the Mosaic law. For the most part, the local cultures that surrounded Israel were considered unclean and unholy. This shift made it necessary for them to join the cultural grouping of Israel—regardless of where they came from.

Even if cultural exclusion and destruction is not the aim of God in Jesus—as we know it is not—the rest of the Old Testament brings us down a difficult path. As we walk it, we must remember that Christ is coming to fulfill the Law and clarify what God means by "A blessing to all people of the world!" The Way of Jesus helps us read the entire Old Testament—especially what takes place after Genesis 12—afresh.

TAKEAWAYS

God committed to bless all peoples regardless of human failure.
The covenant with Abram reveals that God decided to bless all the peoples of the world despite sin. Even after establishing the Abrahamic covenant to bless the world, Israel failed to remain faithful to Yahweh. Jesus fulfills this covenant by revealing himself to us regardless of human failure—God sent Jesus to save us. Regardless of our cultural sins and brokenness, Jesus has come to bless us. We must remember God's desire and commitment toward humanity that in the end, God will bless in Christ.

The Way of Jesus clarifies what God means to bless the nations.
The covenant with Abram places us in an uncomfortable part of God's story. Why? God becomes culturally exclusive for much of the Old Testament. Yet we learn from the entire story that God would be fully revealed in the person of Jesus. The

full revelation of God will define for us what is meant by "All the families of the earth shall be blessed" (Genesis 12:3). Jesus was crucified to bring the nations into the plan of God. Jesus was cursed by the crowds to spread his blessing through salvation. Jesus took on the curse of a violent death to reframe our understanding of violence toward the cultural other.

8

CULTURAL EXCLUSION AND VIOLENCE

Deuteronomy 7:1–4

Main point

▶ God used Israel to judge diverse cultural nations.

After God established the Abrahamic covenant, God's people entered hundreds of years of suffering and marginalization. Genesis leads into Exodus, where we read of how the descendants of Abraham were thrown into slavery in Egypt. Scholar Hemchand Gossai notes that the early narrative of Scripture and its characters are "subsumed through voicelessness and abuse."[1] Amid the cultural oppression that Israel experienced, God promises to give Israel a land of their own.

This leads us to consider the difficult passages that highlight the conquest narrative. Let me start with a few important caveats:

First, on this journey we must face all parts of Scripture—not just those that paint a positive picture of cultural identity development. The narrative of Scripture suggests that God used Israel to destroy people made in the image of God. It is hard to understand why God would create all people with inherent worth and then allow those same people to be destroyed. In the process, cultural identities were destroyed as well. We can't ignore these parts of Scripture, and we won't, but we must address them in the context of God's work in Jesus.

Second, no piece of ancient literature lives up to the modern Western understanding of justice, the common good, or individual rights. We must free the Scriptures from the expectation that every page will sit well with our Western logic or feelings. It is also critical to reject the Western principle that *we have an enlightened understanding of justice* and can therefore judge the Bible when we want. While we need to read Scripture with a critical eye, it is better to allow the text to be what it was meant to be—and to make sure we allow Jesus to shape our understanding of the difficult passages.[2]

Most importantly, we must consider where these stories find their resolution. It is okay if these stories are confusing or difficult to accept. We are headed toward Jesus! We are headed toward the new covenant. We are headed to the shores of God's cultural protections in the gospel of Jesus Christ. We will move from cultural conquest to the embrace of the cultural other. The cultural Christ will give every people of the world God's divine response of love. Calvary replaces conquest.

WAR AND CONQUEST

If we start the story when Israel is marching into battle, we've missed some very important context leading up to that point. At the end of Genesis, the people of Israel are living as immigrants in the most powerful nation on the planet, Egypt. Fast-forward years later, and those in power did not like that Israel was flourishing in Egypt. Pharaoh and the Egyptian priests began to fear this immigrant population. In response, Israel suffered through forced labor and inhumane living conditions. This included Egypt murdering nearly every firstborn son in the land of Goshen, where the Israelites were being held captive.

After God rescued Israel from Egypt, Joshua was called to bring Israel into a land of their own. But in this promised land there resided other nations, other peoples, and other cultures. These cultural groupings served other gods, worshiped idols, and mixed their cultural expressions in ways that rejected Yahweh. Regular human sacrifice took place—Molech, a local deity, demanded the sacrifice of a family's firstborn child. If the mother showed any signs of sorrow at the sacrifice, she'd have to sacrifice her next child. Young women and men were forced into cult prostitution where men would sleep with the prostitutes to mimic the sexual union of Baal and Ashtoreth. The rights of the poor were rejected. God had to respond. Let's explore some of these passages together.

Deuteronomy 7:1–2 reads:

> When the LORD your God brings you into the land that you are about to enter and occupy and he clears away many nations before you—the Hittites, the Girgashites, the Amorites, the Canaanites, the Perizzites, the Hivites, and the Jebusites, seven nations more numerous and mightier than you—and when the LORD your God gives them over to you and you defeat them, then you must utterly destroy them.

God identifies seven nations that were serving false gods. These nations lived in the land that God gave Israel. Today, that region includes parts of Lebanon, Jordan, Syria, and Egypt. This land had fertile plains and beautiful valleys. It also possessed mountain ranges, which included the Judean and Samarian Hills. It boasted the Dead Sea, the lowest point on the earth's surface. This diverse and bountiful region is why the Hebrew writers described this land as flowing with milk and honey.

The seven nations listed in Deuteronomy 7:1 were much stronger than Israel. Yet God told his people to destroy and defeat each nation through war.

Deuteronomy 7:2–4 continues:

> Make no covenant with them and show them no mercy. Do not intermarry with them, giving your daughters to their sons or taking their daughters for your sons, for that would turn away your children from following me, to serve other gods.

Here, God instructs Israel to make no bargain nor enter any treaty with the seven pagan nations. God did not want Israel to mix cultural practices. Yahweh didn't want the religious ways of these nations to seep into Israel. Yahweh wanted strict separation in order that Israel engage in true worship and stay away from idolatry. The nations were to receive no mercy or compassion while Israel moved into the promised land.

What were the cultural implications of these verses? Thousands of people were killed. Millions of cultural artifacts were destroyed. Clothes made by seamstresses were burned. Cultural heirlooms were lost. Instruments were smashed. Those speaking foreign languages were killed. Married people lost their spouses. Children lost their parents. Mothers lost their sons. This was ancient Near Eastern warfare through and through. From this passage forward, there are many instances of God commanding Israel through the prophets to wage violent conquest on foreign nations. Every time this happens, local cultures and people are destroyed in the process.

Sodom and Gomorrah (Genesis 18:20–21; 19:24–25)

God destroys the cities of Sodom and Gomorrah because they engaged in false worship. The story of the residents wanting to have sexual relations with the visitors is based on documented practices in Sodom and Gomorrah, where travelers would be stripped naked and abused for the pleasure of the cities' elite. These cities were also known to be gluttonous and for failing to care for the poor (Ezekiel 16:49–50).

Plagues on Egypt (Exodus 7–12)

God liberates Israel from slavery by destroying Egypt through many plagues. Each plague was directed at a particular Egyptian god (Exodus 12:12). The plague of frogs, for example, was a direct confrontation of the Egyptian goddess Heqtit, who was portrayed as a woman with a frog's head. The final plague, the killing of the firstborns, was both an answer to the genocide of the Israelite people and a statement to Pharoah— who believed himself to be an incarnation of a god—that not even his own son was safe.

The Conquest of Jericho (Joshua 6)

God uses Israel to destroy the city of Jericho during the violent conquest of Canaan. Jericho was a major fortified city on the outskirts of Canaan. According to Rahab, a resident of Jericho, her people knew of Yahweh and how he had defeated the Egyptian gods, but Jericho refused to acknowledge or worship

Yahweh. After Joshua and the people marched around the city for seven days, God caused the walls to fall, and the armies of Israel destroyed everything.

From these stories we learn that false worship has a cost. Sin corrupts culture and demands a divine response.[3] Yet the cultural consequences were devastating. The unique cultural expressions of non-Jewish peoples were crushed. While the divine response of the Old Testament seems to take the form of brutal violence, bloodshed, and destruction of local cultures in the name of God, God's response in the New Testament was to send Jesus Christ to take on the cost of false worship. We also learn from the New Testament that Jesus continues the theme of judgment toward those who reject the good news of Jesus. While the offer of salvation is available to all people who believe in the sacrifice of God in Christ, ultimate judgment will come when Jesus returns.[4]

TAKEAWAYS

There are divine consequences for sin and false worship.

In the Old Testament narrative, God uses armies, natural disasters, and divine intervention to punish those who reject Yahweh. We also see that God consistently remained long-suffering toward the nations until justice became the appropriate response to continued human rebellion. Then, in Christ, the consequences for human sin were satisfied on the cross to bring the nations back to God. The gospel of Jesus is the solution to the problem of false worship.

The Way of Jesus casts a light over violent conquest and cultural exclusion.

Where the Old Testament paints a picture of God's judgment toward all cultures outside of Israel, the fullness of God's plan is revealed in Christ. While we should never dismiss these Old Testament passages, we must cast the light of Jesus over the violence. This means understanding God's ultimate will as it is expressed in Jesus' cross-bearing love. We must understand these passages while considering Jesus' teaching to love our cultural neighbors as we would our own family.

The Way of Jesus does not include destroying people on behalf of God.

So many Christian groups throughout church history have used these passages to justify war, execution, murder, or forms of interpersonal violence against minority groups. The slaughter of Indigenous peoples in the Americas. Canadian residential schools, many of them operated by churches, that stole the culture, and sometimes lives, of Indigenous children. The transatlantic slave trade. These were all done by people using the conquest narratives in the Old Testament to justify cultural and human destruction. When we read these passages in light of Jesus, we see that Jesus teaches us to never use violence against culturally vulnerable family members, neighbors, or nations, including our enemies.

9

JEWISH MINORITIES IN EXILE

Daniel and Esther

Main point

▶ The Israelites modeled cultural resistance while living as Jewish minorities in exile.

After Israel went into the promised land, they struggled to follow God's Law. They failed to follow the Ten Commandments, they worshiped foreign gods, they built idols, and they adopted political structures similar to those of neighboring nations. God's people failed to protect the widow, orphan, and foreigner. As a result, they bore the brunt of the curses set out in Deuteronomy 28: "But if you will not obey the LORD your God by diligently observing all his commandments and decrees that I am commanding you today, then all these curses shall come upon you and overtake you . . ." (v. 15). Israel was scattered from their land and entered a long, painful exile.

During exile, followers of Yahweh became cultural minorities who were forced to adapt to hostile lands and culturally different spaces. The questions during exile became, How do we follow Yahweh as a cultural minority? Can an Israelite be faithful to God while learning new languages? Is it possible to be faithful to God while unable to live in Israel and follow all aspects of the Mosaic law? These questions are the backdrop to two important stories that foreshadow Jesus' minority experience in the first century. In the books of Daniel and Esther, we learn about the postures of cultural resistance and adaptation in hostile lands. These two stories reveal God's blessing on these scattered followers in exile as they navigated their cultural heritage with the demands and dangers of environments that were often hostile to Judaism.

THE STORY OF DANIEL

The book of Daniel was written about six hundred years before Jesus' birth during a dark moment in Jewish history. It captures the experiences of the Israelites during the Babylonian exile, after Babylon conquered Jerusalem in 586 BCE. In ancient times of conquest, it was customary to kill or take captive the royal educator class of those you conquered. In this case, Daniel and others were taken captive and transported to Babylon.

In the capital of Babylon, they were robbed of their ability to practice the Mosaic law as God intended. They were forcibly immersed in Babylonian culture—educated in its language and literature and forced to serve at the royal court. In the early pages of Daniel, we see his counterparts Hananiah, Mishael, and Azariah stripped of their given Jewish names and given the Babylonian names Shadrach, Meshach, and Abednego. This is an example of the forced cultural assimilation the Jewish people underwent in exile. The book serves not only as a historical account but also as a literary piece that encourages faithfulness to God amid cultural oppression, promoting hope in God's ultimate justice and deliverance. The book also points to Jesus as the Son of Man who will liberate and vindicate those faithful to follow Yahweh across world history.

Direct cultural resistance: Daniel 6:10–23

By the time we arrive at chapter 6, Daniel is an important political figure in the royal courts of Babylon. Yet Daniel is faced with a life-threatening situation when King Darius enacts a new law that prohibits prayer to any god except the king for thirty days. While Daniel is protected by his status, he faces a very difficult decision in this foreign land. Would he follow the unjust laws of the land? Would he pray in secret, or would he openly defy the law and pray to Yahweh?

We read Daniel's response to this cultural and ethical dilemma in Daniel 6:10:

> Although Daniel knew that the document [enforcing the prohibition] had been signed, he continued to go to his house, which had windows in its upper room open toward Jerusalem, and to get down on his knees three times a day to pray to his God and praise him, just as he had done previously.

Daniel remains steadfast in his faith and continues his routine of praying three times a day to God, openly defying the edict. The enemies of Daniel catch him praying and bring him before the king, who reluctantly orders Daniel be thrown into the lions' den. Despite his personal regard for Daniel, Darius is compelled to enforce the law.

> At dawn, the king got up and at first light hurried to the den of lions. When he came near the den where Daniel was,

he cried out anxiously to Daniel, "O Daniel, servant of the living God, has your God whom you faithfully serve been able to deliver you from the lions?" Daniel then said to the king, "O king, live forever! My God sent his angel and shut the lions' mouths so that they would not hurt me, because I was found blameless before him; also before you, O king, I have done no wrong." (vv. 19–21)

God honors Daniel's obedience to Yahweh in openly resisting the assimilationist laws of Babylon, miraculously protecting him from the hungry lions. Overjoyed, Darius decrees that Daniel's God should be revered, acknowledging God's power and deliverance.

This story is rich with cultural significance, reflecting how challenging it can be to live a life true to your culture while being expected to abandon your religious heritage. In this narrative, Daniel's commitment to his religious practices amid a Babylonian empire that sought to enforce uniformity through its laws showcases the tension between political authority and personal faith. Daniel's actions—continuing to pray to God despite the decree from King Darius—highlight his defiance against assimilation into the prevailing cultural norms that conflicted with his devout Jewish identity.

The political intrigue that leads to Daniel's punishment also reveals the complexities of navigating faith in an environment where politics and religion are intertwined, often to the detriment of minority people. His subsequent survival in the lion's den is not just a personal miracle but a powerful statement about the supremacy of Daniel's God over the gods of Babylon and the earthly power of the king. This story served as a profound message to the Jewish diaspora about God's ability to protect and favor those who remain loyal in their faith, even under oppressive circumstances.

Cultural identity reflections

Daniel and his friends were outsiders immersed in an unfamiliar Babylonian culture, given new names, and educated in the ways of the Babylonians (Daniel 1:3–7). Like many minority Christians today, they also faced the difficulty of engaging with this culture without losing their Jewish identity and faith. Daniel chose a tactful approach to the challenging task of refusing the king's food, proposing a test to demonstrate that a diet in accordance with Jewish law would not harm them (1:8–14). This shows his diplomatic skills and respect for authority while adhering to his convictions. Daniel was clearly pushing the cultural limits in hostile territory. His rise to power threatened other high-ranking officials, leading to plots against him (Daniel 6). His ability to navigate these political waters, maintain his integrity, and remain committed to God underscores the complexity of his position.

Both of these stories in Daniel highlight God's blessing on Jewish minorities who refused to bend the knee to cultural and religious assimilationist expectations in Babylon. For the millions of Christians around the world being asked to set aside their cultural and faith-based practices amid dominant cultural situations, Daniel's example in exile is a reminder that God cares about minority culture and expression. These passages make clear that God allows Christians to engage in cultural resistance in spaces where people expect them to assimilate or give up their home culture altogether.

THE STORY OF ESTHER

The book of Esther is set in the Persian Empire during the reign of King Ahasuerus, who ruled from 486 to 465 BCE. The narrative unfolds in the Persian capital of Susa. God's people had ended up in Persia as part of the Jewish diaspora after the Babylonian captivity. Cyrus the Great conquered Babylon, which meant that the Persian Empire inherited the territories that included the Jewish exiles. Esther, the main character in this book, appears to have been raised in the care of her cousin Mordecai after being orphaned. In the book, God uses this vulnerable Jewish orphan living in a foreign land to save her people from genocide.

Creative cultural resistance

The story begins after King Ahasuerus dismisses the previous queen, Vashti, for disobedience. In her place, the Israelite Esther is chosen for her beauty to be the new queen. Esther 2:10 says, "Esther did not reveal her people or kindred, for Mordecai had charged her not to tell." While it is unclear exactly why Esther did this, her discretion helped protect her from cultural prejudice and possibly lessened existing tensions or biases against Jews in the Persian Empire. In the story, the concealment of her ethnic identity gives her a strategic advantage that would be used for the good of her people.

After some time, the king's advisor Haman plots to kill all the Jews in the empire because of his personal vendetta against Esther's cousin Mordecai. Mordecai discovers the plot and urges Esther to intervene.

Esther's response to Mordecai is recorded in Esther 4:15–5:2:

> "Go, gather all the Jews to be found in Susa, and hold a fast on my behalf, and neither eat nor drink for three days, night or day. I and my maids will also fast as you do. After that I will go to the king, though it is against the law, and if I perish, I perish." . . .

On the third day Esther put on her royal robes and stood in the inner court of the king's palace, opposite the king's hall. The king was sitting on his royal throne inside the palace opposite the entrance to the palace. As soon as the king saw Queen Esther standing in the court, she won his favor, and he held out to her the golden scepter that was in his hand. Then Esther approached and touched the top of the scepter.

In response to the imminent genocide of her people, Esther instructs her cousin to direct her people in Susa to pray and fast for three days. These religious practices were often done when asking God for wisdom, in times of transition, or in a season of great need. Esther even enlists her maids to join her fellow Israelites in prayer. This is an example of Esther's creative resistance as a follower of Yahweh in hostile cultural territory.

The beginning of chapter 5 indicates that Esther approaches her husband and king strategically. Esther wears Persian clothing and follows the cultural protocols required for approaching the king, even touching the golden scepter. While these acts could be seen as mixing pagan culture with her faith, Esther does this carefully, with great intention. She follows the Persian cultural norms as she advances toward her husband in order to secure the favor she is looking to receive in the situation. This passage demonstrates Esther's strategic courage and the tension between two competing needs: hidden identity and advocacy on behalf of one's own cultural group. Her decision to risk her life by approaching the king uninvited underscores the complexities of identity, power, and responsibility in a cultural minority context.

Esther asks King Ahasuerus if she can hold a banquet for her husband and Haman. At that banquet she invites them to yet another banquet, and at that banquet, Esther reveals her Jewish identity and accuses Haman of plotting to exterminate her people, leading to Haman's execution.

> The king and Haman went in to feast with Queen Esther. On the second day, as they were drinking wine, the king again said to Esther, "What is your petition, Queen Esther? It shall be granted you. And what is your request? Even to half of my kingdom, it shall be fulfilled." Then Queen Esther answered, "If I have won your favor, O king, and if it pleases the king, let my life be given me—that is my petition—and the lives of my people—that is my request. For we have been sold, I and my people, to be destroyed, to be killed, and to be annihilated. If we had been sold merely as slaves, men and women, I would have held my peace, but no enemy can compensate for this damage to the king." Then King Ahasuerus said to Queen Esther, "Who is he, and where is he, who has presumed to do this?" Esther said, "A foe and an enemy, this wicked Haman!" Then Haman was terrified before the king and the queen. (7:1–6)

Despite the risk to her own life, Esther reveals her Jewish heritage to the king and exposes Haman's plot. These verses reveal Esther's cultural intelligence in responding to Haman's violence toward her people while trying to win over her husband to protect her people. While Queen Esther could not predict the outcome of the situation, she positions herself, as wife, queen, and minority Jewish person, to do her best to advocate for the Israelites from her position of power in a pagan government system.

Then, taking a step beyond her first leap of faith to defend her people, she openly calls out Haman. This further puts

Esther in a vulnerable position if the king will side with his advisor.

Moved by her courage, the king grants permission to the Jews to defend themselves against their attackers. The Jews prevail, Haman is executed, and Mordecai is elevated to a position of high honor. The story culminates in the establishment of the festival of Purim to celebrate Jewish deliverance, highlighting themes of courage, faith, and divine providence in the face of adversity.

This story powerfully highlights themes of ethnic tension, the use of power for justice, and the pivotal role of individual agency in effecting change. This creative cultural resistance brought justice in an unlikely situation where the orphaned girl-turned-queen of Persia was able to defend her people from the further loss of cultural identity through a violent genocide.

Cultural identity reflections

Esther initially hid her Jewish heritage—a choice reflecting the dangers and challenges of minority existence within the Persian Empire (Esther 2:10). But her eventual disclosure of her identity to save her people demonstrates the pivotal role that identity can play in cultural and political dynamics. Furthermore, Esther skillfully navigated her limited agency as a woman in a patriarchal society. Her strategic use of her position and her relationship with King Ahasuerus reveal the nuanced ways in which unequal power dynamics can be leveraged for good (5:1–8). Haman's plot to exterminate the Jews highlights the extreme ethnic prejudices of the time. Esther's story is a testament to the resilience and agency of minorities in the face of systemic oppression (3:5–6; 7:3–6). And finally, the use of banquets and fasts in Esther's story reflects the cultural significance of these activities in shaping and shifting political and social narratives (4:16; 5:4–8). From beginning to end, Esther is a riveting story of creative cultural resistance by a minority woman in exile.

The stories of Esther and Daniel, both set against the backdrop of imperial powers, show how individuals from a minority culture navigate their identities, influence their societies, and remain faithful to God. They highlight the importance of wisdom, courage, and culturally informed strategic action in confronting and transforming cultural and political structures. These two Old Testament examples push the limits of what it means to follow Yahweh in foreign lands and navigate pagan cultural customs while remaining faithful to the Law. Like many Christians in the world today, Esther and Daniel stand as important examples of cultural resistance to dominant structures and cultural practices that threaten the very good image of God given to those in difficult cultural situations.

TAKEAWAYS

Daniel, like Jesus, refused to assimilate to dominant cultural practices.

Jesus is the ultimate representation of Daniel to humanity. Jesus, like Daniel, teaches us the importance of maintaining our integrity and cultural practices, even when faced with cultural pressures that contradict our beliefs. Jesus perfectly followed the Old Testament Law while resisting the cultural syncretism of the ruling Jewish class of his day. Jesus remained politically faithful to his Father amid Roman occupation and the constant pressures of the Pharisees and Sadducees. Followers of Jesus in each generation are called to remain faithful to the Way of Jesus when dominant culture presses in.

*Esther, like Jesus, strategically and creatively used her cultural
identity for the greater good.*

Jesus is the ultimate representation of Esther to humanity.
Jesus, like Esther, used his position and cultural identity
to advocate for the salvation of his people—in his case, all
humankind. Esther points to the advocacy that God offered in
sending the cultural Christ to die to protect all peoples in the
world. The unveiling of the gospel in Christ should inspire us
to consider how we might use our own positions—whether
professional roles, cultural identities, or social statuses—to
advocate for justice and protect the vulnerable. In practical
terms, this could mean using one's influence in the workplace
to foster inclusivity, standing up for colleagues who face dis-
crimination, or leveraging one's cultural understanding to
bridge divides and build community in diverse settings.

*Jesus shows us how to follow God in culturally hostile lands with
expectations of assimilation.*

Jesus navigated a landscape that was not only religiously
diverse but also hostile to rabbi-ship and cultural identity.
Jesus shows us how to engage with the culture around us as he
navigated the nuances of speaking with tax collectors, Roman
soldiers, Samaritans, women, and children. This teaches us to
engage with our own cultures thoughtfully. Jesus teaches us
to refuse assimilation in areas where the cultural identity that
God has given us is threatened.

10

GLIMMERS OF CULTURAL INCLUSION

1 Kings 17:8–15; 2 Kings 5:1–14

Main point

▶ The prophets give glimpses of the cultural dignity that Jesus will bring.

I have a bad case of insomnia. Ever since I can remember, I've had trouble falling asleep. Even now, I'm writing these words at 2:28 on a Sunday morning. Worse still, I gave my insomnia to my firstborn daughter Aahana! When she was a newborn, I would walk with her for over an hour around eleven each night as she very slowly fell asleep. Right now, Aahana is up with me drawing on the couch while I'm writing on my computer.

A few years ago while staying at a house in northern Idaho, Aahana came out of her room to see whether I was still awake. It was nearly five in the morning. I had stayed up all night and decided to watch the sunrise and take some photos. She smiled at me as if to say, "You're awake too!" I asked her to grab a sweatshirt so we could go outside in the cold early morning. The house was on a ridge overlooking a valley—on a clear day you could see houses, hundreds of trees, and a winding river that cut through the flat landscape leading into a lake. We quietly opened the sliding door and stepped outside onto the ice-cold ground. Still one hour from sunrise, it was so dark we could barely see in front of our faces. We watched as the breeze of the morning slowly pushed and pulled the fog around us.

When the landscape went from pitch-dark to faint light, Aahana asked me, "Where is the light coming from?" While Aahana recognized it was not dark anymore, it wasn't clear to her what was producing the light. This strange period before the sun comes up is called twilight. "Right now, you can't see it, but the sun is producing this soft blue light all around us," I said. Aahana gave a big, tired smile. After another ten minutes it became clear where the light was coming from as a soft orange color rose over one side of the sky. We went back into the house, and about an hour later, we watched the sun rise through the eastern ridge in the distance.

THE DARK NIGHT OF CULTURAL EXCLUSION

In our Old Testament survey, we have learned that Israel engaged in a holy conquest that resulted in the cultural destruction of various people groups. The effects of sin were felt across the world. False worship led to judgment. The judgment of God on foreign nations was devastating on all levels. God also brought punishment on Israel for engaging in false worship and abandoning the Law. Things were murky and foggy. It looked like Israel would never be the cultural blessing that God had promised Abram in Genesis 12. But

God provided a sacrificial system so his people could receive forgiveness and be restored.

Even then, Israel did not stay true to God. After decades of patient long-suffering, Yahweh took the fractured nation of Israel off into captivity to discipline his people. Israel found itself a cultural minority fighting to maintain a cultural identity that the people had taken for granted. The night had set in.

THE HOPE OF TWILIGHT

Even within the darkest moments of the Old Testament, there were faint signs of twilight. We find stories about cultural inclusion that foreshadow the coming of the cultural inclusion found in the gospel of Jesus Christ. Although Israel could not yet see the coming light of Christ, hints and glimmers of the cultural inclusion that he would usher in appear. While Israel largely embodied a spirit of cultural domination, exclusion, and destruction, these small stories of cultural inclusion signaled that the sun would one day rise.

While I do not have space to survey all the incredible stories that foreshadow the cultural inclusion that God would bring in Jesus, I want to explore two critical stories that signal the coming sun. In the opening of his ministry, Jesus cites both of these stories: the story of the widow of Zarephath in 1 Kings 17 and the healing of Naaman in 2 Kings 5. In both stories, important Jewish prophets go beyond their duty to Israel to welcome non-Jewish enemies into God's loving embrace. The first story highlights a Jewish prophet entering a foreign country to dignify a poor Gentile widow. The second story focuses on a rich Gentile warrior entering a foreign land to culturally humble himself before God. Both draw out the posture that followers of Jesus are to have before God as we develop our cultural identity.

THE CROSS-CULTURAL LOVE OF ELIJAH

In 1 Kings 17, Israel finds itself in a horrible famine and intense drought that affected the entire ancient Near East. Elijah was a prophet called by God to speak on behalf of Yahweh during this time. It was Elijah's central concern to protect, provide, and speak truth to Israel. In this passage, God tells Elijah to embark on a cross-cultural journey to the land of Sidon, an enemy nation outside of Israel. The people of Sidon held a different cultural identity—they spoke a different language, had different cultural customs, sang different songs, and worshiped different gods.

> The word of the LORD came to [Elijah], saying, "Go now to Zarephath, which belongs to Sidon, and live there, for I have commanded a widow there to feed you." So he set out and went to Zarephath. (1 Kings 17:8–10)

Zarephath was a Phoenician city in what is now modern-day Lebanon. The surrounding region of Sidon was an economic hub. It was a place of cultural intersections and service to many different gods. This area was culturally diverse and would have been hit hard by the famine and drought. With this command to Elijah, a Jewish prophet, to live in this Gentile city within a Gentile nation, God was asking Elijah to live as a cultural minority. Elijah became a traveler who needed to learn the ways of the people that surrounded him. Elijah's posture in Sidon is in stark contrast with the conquest narratives that we considered in the previous chapter.

While Elijah was in Zarephath, God wanted the prophet to meet with a widow—a person of very low social class. Elijah found the widow and told her to bring him water and bread. This was no small ask in a time when many people were dying of starvation and thirst.

[The widow] said, "As the LORD your God lives, I have nothing baked, only a handful of meal in a jar and a little oil in a jug; I am now gathering a couple of sticks so that I may go home and prepare it for myself and my son, that we may eat it and die." (v. 12)

In this culture, widows were especially vulnerable to poverty. In times of drought or famine, if no one was watching over widows, they would be the first to suffer. This story indicates that she was in extreme danger of losing her life or watching her son die.

Thankfully, she encountered Elijah, who responded to her horrifying situation with these words:

Do not be afraid; go and do as you have said, but first make me a little cake of it and bring it to me, and afterwards make something for yourself and your son. For thus says the LORD the God of Israel: The jar of meal will not be emptied and the jug of oil will not fail until the day that the LORD sends rain on the earth. (vv. 13–14)

With this confusing command, Elijah was telling this desperate widow that God would perform an ongoing miracle in order to sustain her through this famine and drought.

This text has many cultural implications. Elijah crossed into enemy cultural territory to live and be with the people in a time of crisis. In this particular interaction, the prophet of Yahweh humbled himself to receive food from a Gentile widow, who was considered unclean. This woman came from a different cultural background, a different religion, and a different class. Elijah was powerful. The widow was powerless. Elijah was Jewish. The widow was Gentile. How did the widow respond to Elijah's prompt?

She went and did as Elijah said, so that she as well as he
and her household ate for many days. (v. 15)

In following Elijah's suggestion, the widow was able to
make food from what little she had to feed Elijah and her son,
and as promised, still the oil and flour did not run out. God
had given the widow the miracle of food in order that she
sustain her house for a long time. In this text, we see the light
of cross-cultural love—a glimmer of Jesus in Elijah's cultural
posture toward a foreign family of an extremely low class.

In this passage, Elijah—
Sat at the table of the cultural other.
Dignified the food of the cultural other.
Left his cultural home for a foreign place.
Honored the language of the Gentile widow.
Lived among those with cultural differences.
Brought a poor woman into the embrace of God.
Shared the power of God with a suffering family.

Instead of laying waste to the culture of Zarephath—
God sent his prophet to dignify the widow.

Instead of commanding God's army to destroy Sidon—
God brought a messenger with cultural compassion.

Instead of bringing violence to those outside of God's land—
God brought a warm cultural embrace into a foreign land.

In this passage, we see the light of Jesus before he was born.
We see God trading cultural exclusion for cultural dignity.

THE CULTURAL HUMILITY OF NAAMAN

This second story takes place a little after the story of Elijah's
care toward the Gentile widow. Leading up to 2 Kings 4, the

author focuses on the military campaign of Israel and the transition from the ministry of Elijah to Elisha.

We pick up in 2 Kings 5:1:

> Naaman, commander of the army of the king of Aram, was a great man and in high favor with his master because by him the LORD had given victory to Aram. The man, though a mighty warrior, suffered from a skin disease.

Naaman, a commander in the land of what is now Syria, held significant influence and wealth, despite suffering from what may have been Hansen's disease, a disease affecting the skin and nerves. In Naaman's day, this condition would have led to potential isolation and death. Despite his high social status, his medical condition threatened to erode his standing and eventually exclude him from his culture.

> Now the Arameans on one of their raids had taken a young girl captive from the land of Israel, and she served Naaman's wife. She said to her mistress, "If only my lord were with the prophet who is in Samaria! He would cure him of his skin disease." So Naaman went in and told his lord just what the girl from the land of Israel had said. And the king of Aram said, "Go, then, and I will send along a letter to the king of Israel." (2 Kings 5:2–5)

This young Jewish girl had been kidnapped and stolen as a result of a military engagement between the Arameans and Israel. The kidnapping and forced slavery of women and children was commonplace in ancient warfare, but that certainly didn't make it any less horrific for those who experienced it. Yet despite her own oppression and displacement, the girl expressed care for her captor. In telling the wife of Naaman that she knew a prophet in Israel who had the power to heal, she displayed cultural care and the desire to love the cultural other even when Naaman did not deserve her kindness.

In response to this news, Naaman sent a letter to the king of Israel inquiring if he could visit Elisha, a Jewish prophet called by God to guide Israel and advise the king. This was because Naaman would need permission to go into a foreign land to be healed. Israel's king tore his clothes, thinking the Aramean commander Naaman was looking to create problems for him. But Elisha didn't share his same suspicions.

> Elisha sent a messenger to [Naaman], saying, "Go, wash in the Jordan seven times, and your flesh shall be restored, and you shall be clean." But Naaman became angry and went away, saying, "I thought that for me he would surely come out and stand and call on the name of the LORD his God and would wave his hand over the spot and cure the skin disease!" . . . [Naaman] turned and went away in a rage. (2 Kings 5:10–12)

Naaman was upset because of unmet cultural expectations. He anticipated a public greeting from Elisha, which was customary when a religious leader met a high-ranking commander. Furthermore, Elisha instructed Naaman to go to the river without his presence, which contradicted the typical expectations that a healer or priest must be present for such miracles. Disappointed, Naaman left, but his men persuaded him to return and follow through with the instructions. Naaman eventually agreed to go back to the water and follow Elisha's instructions.

> He went down and immersed himself seven times in the Jordan, according to the word of the man of God; his flesh

was restored like the flesh of a young boy, and he was clean. (2 Kings 5:14)

Naaman humbled himself even though God gave him instructions that didn't match his cultural expectations. He had to adjust what he expected to match what God wanted. Naaman entered a space of cultural humility while entering foreign water, in a foreign country, and under the direction of a foreign religious leader. He set aside his cultural practices and his own views of God by traveling to enemy territory on the chance of receiving God's embrace. God was patient with Naaman while he wrestled with his own pride and cultural closed-mindedness. Where the conquest stories reveal a God fed up with sin and false worship, this story reveals the soft and warm embrace of Yahweh, who gave this man another chance.

These two stories highlight the light of Christ during the dark days of Israel. God sent the prophets into the world to signal the greater prophet to come who would clarify how God would relate to culture, cultural identity, and the nations.

TAKEAWAYS

Jesus, like Elijah, humbly came to heal us in our cultural settings.
Elijah reveals the lengths that God will go to share love with those made in God's image. God is calling us to focus on the embrace that Elijah extended to a widow who was suffering with her son in Sidon. When considering your own life, how is God extending this love and embrace toward you? Are you willing to listen to God even when it does not make sense or feels strange? It took faith for the Gentile widow to listen to and follow a foreign Jewish prophet in a time when everything was on the line. We must open our hearts and cultural identities to a God who has come to us like Elijah.

Jesus, like Elisha, expects us to come to God for salvation and cultural enlightenment.

While Elijah shows us that God comes to us in times of need, the story with Elisha reveals the necessity that we come to God for healing. Elisha calls us, like Naaman, to the waters of God to be healed. We can't let pride, or our own experiences, stop us from coming to the powerful healing of God in Christ. We must come to Jesus. We must make the journey, like Naaman, to a place of discomfort to form our true cultural identity. What areas of your cultural identity do you need to humbly place before God? What areas of your own culture is God asking you to set aside to enter the Way of Jesus?

Part III

NEW TESTAMENT AND CULTURE

11

THE CULTURAL CHRIST

John 1:9–14

Main point

▶ God is revealed as the Jewish Savior, born a suffering cultural minority.

In the tension of the Old Testament, the prophet Habakkuk writes, "How long, LORD, must I call for help, but you do not listen? Or cry out to you, 'Violence!' but you do not save?" (Habakkuk 1:2 NIV). Through the cries of suffering bodies and destroyed cultures, God answered in the form of Jesus Christ. Amid the tears of the oppressed and hurting, God came down to be among God's people. This is the incarnation. This is our cultural Christ.

We will start our New Testament survey in the gospel of John. In chapter 1, John connects Jesus all the way back to Genesis.

The true light, which enlightens everyone, was coming into the world.

He was in the world, and the world came into being through him, yet the world did not know him. He came to what was his own, and his own people did not accept him. (John 1:9–11)

John begins by asserting that Jesus is for everyone. Regardless of your age, gender, sexual identity, ethnicity, or any other cultural marker, Jesus is the path you should follow. Our cultural identity is found only in our true light, Jesus. Cultural enlightenment comes only through Christ.

Verse 10 explains that Jesus created the very world he was born into. God created the very nation he inhabited. The world that God designed to contain an array of cultural perspectives was graced by Jesus. We further learn that God came to earth but was not recognized by the people he created. Though God came to earth and wore the same clothes as his chosen people, shared their same space, spoke their language, and came from a well-known Jewish tribe, many Israelites didn't recognize the authority of Jesus. Many of the people whom God came to live among, the Israelites, did not accept Jesus. Even though God joined humanity and incarnated in a cultural location like us, many of Jesus' own people—and many Romans—rejected him.

John 1 continues:

But to all who received him, who believed in his name, he gave power to become children of God, who were born, not of blood or of the will of the flesh or of the will of man, but of God. (vv. 12–13)

Verse 12 pivots with the conjunction *but*. This *but* is meant to contrast the rejection that Jesus experienced on earth with the acceptance that God shows those who receive Christ. The gospel is the good news that Christ has physically died for the world and resurrected to offer us a second chance. A third chance. A tenth chance!

All people experience brokenness. All cultures are full of good and bad. All individuals, no matter the nuances of their cultural identity, need saving and forgiveness for their sins. We all need to be fully restored in the purposes given to our ancestors through Adam and Eve. We need to relearn how to display the imago Dei in the world. In order to restore us, Jesus came to give us the right to become a child of God regardless of our cultural location. Did you hear that?!

> From Tagalog or Spanish—
> Jesus died for you.
> With national pride or without any nation—
> Jesus is your land.
> From refugee or multigenerational landowner—
> Jesus is your safety.
> From east or distant west—
> Jesus extends forgiveness to your people.
> Whether minority or majority culture—
> Jesus was crucified to save you.
> High-class, low-class, or in-between class—
> Jesus resurrected for you.
> Those confused or clear about culture—
> the Jewish Jesus offers you salvation.
>
> Each culture,
> all bodies,
> every class,
> all language,
> every nation,
> every age bracket,

and every ethnicity
has been given the
chance to self-adopt
into God's family.

There is *no* cultural elitism with Jesus.

All have been given the right to be in God's family.

John 1:14 continues:

And the Word became flesh and lived among us, and we
have seen his glory, the glory as of a father's only son, full
of grace and truth.

Jesus, the Word, became human! The second person of the
Trinity entered the time-space universe in the form of a Jewish
man in first-century Palestine.

God became a(n)—
Ethnic Jew.
Member of the Oppressed class.
Political threat.
Gendered male.
Occupied body.
Minority person.
Member of Israel.
Refugee to Egypt.
Hebrew speaker.
Carpenter and rabbi.
Incarcerated minority.
Son to Mary and Joseph.

The Jewish Messiah—
king over all.

The complex, specific cultural background of Christ was the means of providing grace and truth to a fragmented world. God sent Jesus to show us how to embody a particular culture in a way that honors God and reflects the image of God in the world. The cultural Christ became the north star for anyone looking to develop their own identity in the world.

Jesus Christ Cultural Matrix

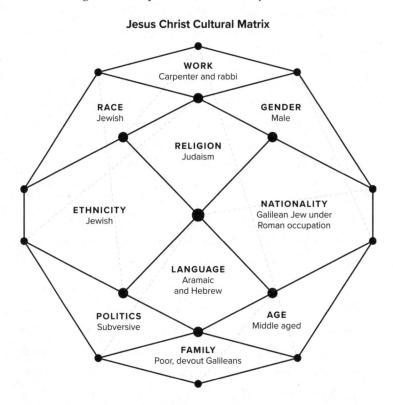

This is the *word made flesh*! God met human culture at the intersections of a mixed ethnic background. In the Gospels, the genealogies of Jesus include non-Israelite figures such as Tamar and Rahab the Canaanites, Ruth the Moabite, and Bathsheba, who may have been a Hittite. While Jesus came from the tribe of Judah in the line of David, these powerful and often marginalized women from the Old Testament highlight the complex and beautiful ethnic blend of Jesus Christ. God was pleased to dwell in the body that carried a variety of ethnic strands. Yet at these ethnic intersections, Jesus was whole, complete, and fully human. The author Chandra Crane notes that, "As a mixed person, Jesus experienced—he embodied—wholeness."[1]

Related to the languages that Jesus spoke, scholar Gosnell L. York writes,

> Jesus himself is known to have spoken Aramaic, his own mother tongue, and not only Hebrew, the language of the Jewish Scriptures but (and if He did at all) also the two dominant languages of his day, namely, the commonly-spoken Greek which was made possible by the colonial exploits and exploitation of Alexander, the Great, who lived and died before His time or Latin, the official language of the conquering Romans—those who ruled the world when He both lived and died; when He uttered His life-changing words and performed His life-changing works.[2]

While many in the United States speak only English, most of the world understands and speaks multiple languages. The learning of multiple languages often springs up out of practical necessity instead of intellectual curiosity or academic requirement. God entered the ancient Near Eastern context where multiple languages were needed as a form of survival under Roman occupation. In this we learn that God was not above cultural adaptation.

We also know that Jesus grew up within a marginalized community. Theologians N. T. Wright and Michael F. Bird write, "In Jesus' world there were constant downward pressures, forcing people toward debt and destitution, and in some cases even toward either banditry or slavery as desperate strategies for survival."[3] God was enculturated into the Hebrew people, who were fighting for a distinct cultural identity under Roman occupation. The profound truth of the incarnation should lead us to worship Jesus and shape our identity around the one who came to save and set us free.

TAKEAWAYS

Jesus dignifies cultural identity.

Jesus, our cultural Christ, learned what it was like to feel pain, hunger, and the struggles of a particular ethnic group. Jesus stood at the crossroads of various Jewish cultures and competing political identities and within a national identity that was fracturing under occupying Roman forces. Our cultural identities have dignity because God has entered the cultural experience in Christ. God in Christ validates our cultural identities by bringing the fullness of God into a cultural location.

Jesus enlightens cultural identity.

For those who adopt the Christian faith, we must look to Jesus for cultural enlightenment. We have the fullness of God's cultural vision in Jesus! What is the implication of this? The fullness of our own cultural identity must be found in Jesus Christ. It is only in community with God that we know who we are, how we should display our culture in the world, and how to live our lives.

Who enlightens our cultural identity? Jesus.
Who brings clarity to our cultural identity? Jesus.
What does God look like on earth? We look to Jesus.
How do we live from our cultural location?
Learn from Jesus.

Jesus validates marginalized cultures.

Jesus was born into the world as a member of a marginalized minority. He was forced to become a refugee to Egypt. He grew up in a family that was overtaxed and unjustly treated. By inhabiting a minority culture in the form of Jesus, God validates the struggle, the pain, and the turmoil felt by millions across the world who find themselves in the same place. Jesus knows what it means to hold a history that is not represented in the books written or stories told within popular culture. In the incarnation, God eternally stands in solidarity and extends sympathy with the peoples of the world fighting from the cultural margins. Just as important, Jesus shows anyone from a minority culture how to resist dominant cultures that surround them.

12

THE GOSPEL FOR ALL CULTURES

Luke 4:17–29

Main point

▶ The gospel of Jesus Christ is meant for all cultures for all time.

In earlier chapters we looked at the sun as a way to think about Jesus. We explored how Christ, like the sun to our planet, gives our cultural identity light and life. The question we will ask in this chapter is, How can Christ's light guide our cultural identity in a more just and beloved direction? What can set our cultural identity straight when we harm others? What has the power to grow our cultural identity to be beautiful?

If Christ is the sun bringing light to earth so we can see, the gospel of Jesus is the sustaining warmth of the sun allowing the land, plants, and creatures to thrive. Without this warmth, plants can't grow. Without this warmth, the world would be an uninhabitable icescape. Likewise, without the power of the gospel, your cultural identity will wither and die. But with the power of the gospel, you can thrive in how God has made you.

Furthermore, the gospel is our moral compass that helps determine how we ought to live out our cultural identity in the world. The gospel is the guide for each culture—regardless of language, nation, ethnic group, or class of people. Now, let's explore the light of the gospel.

CULTURAL BROKENNESS

Every single human has a deep capacity for love, sacrifice, and kindness. In the West we call these qualities virtues, and the Scriptures call them the fruits of God's Spirit. The result of God's good fruit in the world is just living. Children are protected from abuse. Parents speak patiently to their children. Women and men have equal rights. Governments tell their citizens the truth. Pastors extend grace toward those they lead. Humans experience joy amid pain. Art is created to foster a better world. Racism is dismantled at every level of society. Economies create access to resources for those born into a lower class. Animals are not needlessly killed. When we embody love and righteousness in our cultural context, we display God's image in the world. Cultures thrive. You thrive.

Yet every cultural grouping has the capacity for all forms of vice: selfishness, indifference, deceit, rage, abuse, idolatry, and violence. When we commit such acts, we live outside our design. We sin. Human sin presents a great challenge to our cultural identity discovery process. Why? Sin infects all aspects of life—including how we use language, how our families function, how we build nations, and how we take care of people who are suffering.

Every cultural group and every person fails to display God's good image in the world all the time. When this happens, children experience abuse. The elderly are abandoned. Parents lash out toward their children. Friendships splinter because of gossip. Women are valued less than men. Politicians live double lives. Pastors weaponize their authority for pleasure or power. Racism is upheld by those who do not care enough to make change. Economies are run by the rich and powerful at the expense of those without. Animals are abused and abandoned.

Our identity fractures under the weight of sin.

Our cultural background mixes with hurt and pain.

The sins of our people run just as deep as the good caused.

We carry misdeeds and malice within our cultural upbringing.

The problems I've just named exist because we, the collective peoples of the world, have failed to follow God to build a better world. I have failed. You have failed. We need a Savior to come restore us to God, each other, self, and creation. We need a light to break in to the darkness of our own cultural brokenness in order to bring healing into our own lives and across our world.

THE GOSPEL OF JUBILEE

Enter Jesus Christ.

In the gospel of Luke, Jesus opens his ministry by declaring his good news for every people group of the world. While Jesus was declaring this to the nation of Israel first, Luke 4 makes clear that Jesus came to pour good news over every nation and people.

In this passage, Jesus is handed the scroll of Isaiah. Standing in front of a home crowd as a Jewish rabbi, Christ unveils his gospel to Israel.

> He unrolled the scroll and found the place where it was written:
> "The Spirit of the Lord is upon me,
>   because he has anointed me
>   to bring *good news* to the poor.
> He has sent me to proclaim release to the captives
>   and recovery of sight to the blind,
>   to set free those who are oppressed,
> to proclaim the year of the Lord's favor."
>
> And he rolled up the scroll, gave it back to the attendant, and sat down. The eyes of all in the synagogue were fixed on him. Then he began to say to them, "Today this scripture has been fulfilled in your hearing." (Luke 4:17–21, emphasis added)

Those listening to Jesus would have known the passage he was reading. Isaiah speaks about an anointed prophet to come who will bring "the year of the LORD's favor." This Jewish concept is also known as Jubilee. These verses that Jesus reads, from Isaiah 61:1–2, are themselves a callback to Leviticus 25. In Leviticus 25, God commands Israel to let the land rest and the suffering people in Israel be restored within their family, tribe, and nation. This Jubilee, or day of the Lord's favor, offered those who were culturally marginalized a chance at redemption. It was an economic, political, and social reset every fifty years. Debts were cleared, and animals were allowed to rest. Enslaved people, indentured workers, broken families, and shamed individuals were given another chance. Culture was restored to the state that God had intended for the garden of Eden. In Jubilee, God's people would experience peace, prosperity, mutual respect, and harmony across culture.

When Jesus quotes the prophet Isaiah who foretold that a Messiah was coming to fulfill this Jubilee in the world, he is offering a radical interpretation of the Jewish concept of Jubilee. In this declaration, Jubilee is for all people—not just those in Israel. Jubilee is to be extended to every tribe, tongue, and nation. Jubilee means that those who follow God must cross cultures in order to love their neighbor. Then, Jesus rolls up the scroll, hands it back, and says that the words from Isaiah calling back the day of the Lord's favor are fulfilled in him.[1]

SPIRITUAL LIFE AND SOCIAL FLOURISHING

In this reinterpretation of Jubilee, Jesus creates a blueprint for understanding the gospel for all cultures. First, all peoples have access to spiritual life through the gospel of Jubilee. The spiritual corruption passed down from our ancestors Adam and Eve has been overcome by the cross of Christ. Our sins have been forgiven. This is good news! God has not abandoned us but sent Jesus to redeem us. Second, all peoples have access to social flourishing through the gospel of Jubilee. The death and resurrection of Jesus signals a new way of living. Jesus has come to show us the Way. This ancient path creates powerful routes toward cultural enlightenment. We mobilize around our leader Jesus to dignify all peoples, love our neighbor, and share this Jubilee in a hurting world.

The gospel of Jubilee declares that . . .

- those disabled and discarded will be dignified.

- people experiencing cultural powerlessness will be protected.
- ethnic groups vulnerable to mistreatment will be safeguarded.
- all people crushed under the weight of their sin will be forgiven.
- spiritual light and life are to be found only in the cultural Christ.

We continue a few verses later in Luke 4:25–27, where Jesus says this:

> But the truth is, there were many widows in Israel in the time of Elijah, when the heaven was shut up three years and six months and there was a severe famine over all the land; yet Elijah was sent to none of them except to a widow at Zarephath in Sidon. There were also many with a skin disease in Israel in the time of the prophet Elisha, and none of them was cleansed except Naaman the Syrian.

You may recall these two stories from the last chapter in our Old Testament survey. God called both Elijah and Elisha to serve Israel. Both men were meant to speak truth to Israel. Both men were held in high regard among those listening to Jesus. What's important here is that these two stories highlight moments where these prophets loved people who were culturally different from them. This was the dawn of the new covenant. In this covenant we are taught to embrace cultural postures marked by dignity and inclusion.

Jesus draws attention to how Elijah cared for a Gentile widow and her son and highlights a time when Elisha healed a privileged Gentile leaper named Naaman. With this, Jesus was saying: The gospel of Jubilee will expand beyond the bounds of the marginalized Israelites to all cultural groups of the world. The gospel of Jubilee will bring about spiritual life through the forgiveness of sins and social flourishing for all people—regardless of their ethnic background, age, gender, nationality, or class. This good news of Jubilee extends all the way to you today! How did the crowds react to this message for all cultures?

> All in the synagogue were filled with rage. They got up, drove him out of the town, and led him to the brow of the hill on which their town was built, so that they might hurl him off the cliff. (Luke 4:28–29)

The people who grew up with Jesus and who helped raise Jesus reacted to this concept so negatively that they decided to kill him. Why? The gospel of Jubilee was radical. The Son of God came to his own oppressed people and declared that his good news reached beyond Israel. The gospel would dignify not only the Jewish people—it would dignify all people. The gospel of Jubilee offers cultural protections for all who call on the name of Jesus. The gospel was also for all who did not understand Hebrew. It was for people who didn't have access to the temple. It was for people who had never uttered the name of Yahweh.

In a time when resources were scarce, many lived in poverty, and the Jews were in constant threat of further violence from the Romans, it was radical to think beyond the walls of one's own family, and certainly one's own people. It was hard to consider how to spread God's love in Gentile areas when the Israelites were trying to maintain their cultural distinctives. When many of the Jews longed for judgment to befall Rome and its allies, Jesus took the Jewish Jubilee meant for Israel and claimed it was meant for all people. The bringer of the gospel was born in Jewish soil to grow fruits of salvation for every tribe and tongue!

TAKEAWAYS

The gospel dignifies our cultural identity.

Jesus dignified human culture by entering a culturally specific location and then dying to save and redeem us all. God did not consider the body dirty, human feelings uninhabitable, or our daily cultural habits unworthy. Christ entered into the daily rhythms of language learning, eating, sweating, laughing, crying, singing, and the honor/shame context of the ancient Near East. Furthermore, Jesus dignified marginalized cultural groups by living through the same experience on earth. God entered this painful space to validate the experience of those who have suffered and to restore the dignity of those who suffer.

The gospel confronts our cultural identity.

Jesus also came to forgive each person for their sins. No sin is committed outside of culture. We use our hands, minds, feelings, and mouths to do good and evil in the world. Each of us fails to display God's image in how we live. We need redemption. We need reshaping. We need direction. Just as Jesus confronted the cultural identity of the crowds in Luke 4, we must allow Jesus to do the same in our lives. Jesus is the light that not only warms us but pierces the dark places of our hearts to expose sin and evil. We must allow Jesus to interrogate our cultural identity to better love God daily.

The gospel shapes our cultural identity.

We must move throughout our lives with a willingness to let the gospel of Jesus shape our cultural identity. We must remain open to cultural change. We should give Jesus the license to interrogate our cultural biases and blind spots. The Way of Jesus is the path of those who desire true cultural enlightenment.

13

THE GREATEST CULTURAL COMMAND

Luke 10:25–28

Main point

▶ Every person is called to love God and
the cultural other.

I'll warn you up front: this chapter might be a challenge to
read. Let me tell you why. This book is about helping us
develop our cultural identities. This requires some internal
focus. Looking inward and reflecting on your own experiences
is an important part of developing your cultural identity. You
might be thinking, No problem, I think about myself all the
time! The problem with self-focus in the Western world is that
we often put the individual in place of God. We swing so far
to the Western mode of living that we forget that love of God
and neighbor should eclipse self-love. This often manifests
in focusing too much on our cultural preferences. When we
do not interrogate our own cultural blind spots, we worship

our culture. We worship ourselves. If we want to develop a healthy, biblical understanding of our own cultural identities, we have to confront these tendencies. And that can be really difficult. But it's important work. God gives us a piercingly simple command to confront self-worship. And then God calls us to look outward into the frontiers of neighbor love.

THE IDOL OF CULTURAL IDENTITY

Let me illustrate what cultural idolatry looks like in a church setting. My wife and I attended a church in rural Indiana for about six months. Most of the congregants—about 95 percent—were white people, and some were Mexican American immigrants. A set of Western Anglo-Saxon cultural norms pervaded the church. Folks showed up on time, left on time, and were very somber during musical worship. Music in four-part harmony was a big deal. Sermons were practical, and the preaching was emotionally tempered. The church revolved around a set of programs that usually emphasized personal piety and love of family. Evangelism was marked by international missions and a shallow commitment to the areas surrounding the building.

While we enjoyed our time at this church, our family was a bit out of place. When we walked in each week, folks were constantly looking at us to figure out where we came from. I wear skinny jeans and have tattoos. Our kids are brown. Our last name wasn't easily placed among the church attendees. My wife was the only Indo-Guyanese person in a hundred-mile radius. One Sunday, a white woman in her mid-fifties sat down with my wife Sarswatie to have a conversation about church. A few minutes into the conversation she said to my wife, "You know . . . I believe we are close to God when we sit quietly before God. It is important that we worship God in an orderly way. This is true worship. This is how we are close to God." After we arrived home, Sarswatie expressed her confusion and discouragement about the conversation. Why did this woman want to tell her this? Why insist on worshiping God only one way? Where in the Bible does it say that quiet singing is more holy than other forms of singing?

The words of this older white woman revealed her cultural bias. It also revealed the deeper problem of cultural idolatry. The woman placed her cultural values of four-part harmony and quiet expression above what Scripture teaches! After all, what about the majority of the world who express their love of God by arriving to church late and staying all day? What about loud singing and dancing—could this not be true worship? What about crying out to God through the playing of drums and sporadic dance? Without knowing it, this woman was idolizing her Anglo cultural values of timeliness, quiet, and four-part harmony. By telling my brown-skinned wife that a person is nearest to God by expressing their love of God like white people, she communicated that Indo-Guyanese culture was far from God. That my wife's cultural identity was not holy or worth keeping. She communicated that non-Western culture is dirty and unclean. This is an example of a Christian placing an aspect of their culture on the level of Jesus or the Bible.

Cultural idolatry is common both inside and outside the church. We tend to take the most important parts of our cultural identities and allow them to subsume our relationship with Jesus, giving our highest loyalty instead to our nation, ethnic group, political party, generation, or gender identity. When we love any aspect of our cultural identity above Jesus, we fall into the trap of self-worship.

Before we continue, I invite you to reflect on the ways that you have chosen to place your own cultural identity above

Jesus. When have you prized your own life, family, ethnic group, nation, or cultural heritage above God? It is critical to self-reflect on our own self-idolatry as we explore the greatest cultural command.

CULTURAL IDENTITY AND THE GREATEST COMMANDMENT

The Scriptures are constantly pushing humans to reject cultural idols for true worship of God. As we now begin to explore more deeply how Jesus offers a better way, our next text will help us center our cultural identity discovery on Jesus in three ways: It will push us to see our cultural identity as an expression of love toward God. It will compel us to consider how our cultural identity can be a blessing to the cultural other. And we will learn that God desires that we manifest love of God and neighbor through the specific culture in which we reside.

We read in Luke 10:25–28:

> An expert in the law stood up to test Jesus. "Teacher," he said, "what must I do to inherit eternal life?" He said to him, "What is written in the law? What do you read there?" He answered, "You shall love the Lord your God with all your heart and with all your soul and with all your strength and with all your mind and your neighbor as yourself." And he said to him, "You have given the right answer; do this, and you will live."

A group of Jewish teachers was looking to test Jesus with a set of questions. They wanted to know which specific law from the Old Testament was the most important. But they also had ulterior motives. These leaders were looking to stump Jesus and derail his ministry. Jesus' brilliant response—that we ought to love God above all and love our neighbor as ourselves—marked a major cultural transition between the old and new covenant. It also simplified how followers of Jesus are to understand how their faith and culture intersect.

LOVING GOD AND NEIGHBOR IN CONTEXT

We learned from our Old Testament survey that God called Israel to be a cultural light to the nations. Before Jesus, God's people were to love God through participation in the nation of Israel. For Jews, this was much easier, because they were born into the right nation, spoke Hebrew, and grew up with an understanding of the Mosaic law. But what about those outside of Israel? How could they love God? Under the Mosaic law, non-Jewish cultural groups needed to give up much of their cultural identity to love Yahweh.

In the ministry of Jesus, we see Christ fulfilling the Old Testament Law by providing a way to love God and neighbor without becoming Jewish. This was a massive shift from how God did things under the Mosaic law. When Jesus sums up the ethnically specific rules and regulations found in the Mosaic law by saying, "You shall love the Lord your God with all your heart and with all your soul and with all your strength and with all your mind and your neighbor as yourself," he offers up a transcultural command—one that is for every culture and every place of the world.

Revisiting the chart that displays cultural identity across the covenants, we can trace the cultural shifts between the old and new covenants. We can see how Jesus came to restore God's original plan in the Table of Nations. In Genesis 10, we learned that God wanted the descendants of Noah to love God in their own local cultures. Jesus came to set all ethnic groups free to love God and neighbor from within their own cultural identities. Because of the life and death of Christ, non-Jews do not need to convert to Judaism. Gentiles do not need to leave their home country, take on a new nationality, or learn Hebrew. Rather, God has liberated us to express our love of God from within our own skin, our own language, and our own unique cultural expressions.

Cultural Identity across the Covenants

	Old covenant	New covenant
Leadership	Priests, prophets, and kings	King Jesus Christ
Nation	Israel	All nations
Location	Temple in Jerusalem	Temple in all people
Language	Hebrew	All languages
Expressions	Jewish identity Torah, circumcision, feasts, temple, sacrifice	Interethnic identity Faith, baptism, communion, etc.
Covenant faithfulness	Adopt a Jewish cultural identity	Convert who remains in native cultural identity

This new covenant shift has important implications for us as we explore our own cultural identity formation. First, it makes it clear that minority culture Christians do not need to assimilate to a dominant culture to follow Jesus. You can be who you are in your home culture without feeling bad about how God created you. Your language is beautiful. The way you relate to family and community is beloved. Do not let majority culture Christians look down on your way of following Jesus. Second, it is sinful for majority culture Christians to take an old covenant posture toward others. No Christian is allowed to enforce their cultural preferences on other Christians as better or holy. We will dive into this more in forthcoming chapters, but we see the foundations of this principle here.

LOVING GOD THROUGH CULTURAL EXPRESSION

We learn from this passage that the chief goal of our lives is to love and worship God. Consider how you can love God through the various aspects of your identity: ethnicity, age, language, nationality, race, gender, family, work, politics, class, stage of life. How can you harness your ethnic background, the language you speak, your gender, or your socioeconomic status to love Jesus? Consider how you can love Jesus from within your own cultural values:

> For those that are gifted musically—play for Jesus.
> For those who have extra money—spend for Jesus.
> Those working a 9-to-5—work for Jesus.
> For those caring for family—love them for Jesus.
> For those who can cook—make food for Jesus.
> For those who are privileged—share your access for Jesus.
> For those good with words—write for Jesus.
> For those good with their hands—build for Jesus.
> To those who are artists—create beautiful things for Jesus.

The key to knowing whether you are loving Jesus with your cultural expression is exploring the *why* behind what you do. What is motivating you every day? What is motivating you to further explore your cultural identity? Jesus teaches us in Luke 10 that God must be at the center of our *why*. Paul writes in 1 Corinthians 10:31, "Whether you eat or drink or whatever you do, do everything for the glory of God." In this verse, Paul pinpoints the common cultural practice of eating as a rightful expression of worship. The way we dress, the food we eat, the words we use, and the way we interact with others should be acts of worship toward Jesus. We must love Jesus through every aspect of our cultural identity.

CULTURAL EXPRESSION AS NEIGHBOR LOVE

After Jesus answers the question by summarizing the Law, the teachers probe Jesus further. A legal expert in the Law asks in Luke 10:29, "Who is my neighbor?" Jesus goes on to tell the story called the parable of the good Samaritan. In this story, Jesus defines *neighbor* as the cultural outsider.

Question: How do I know if I am loving and worshiping God daily?

Answer: Loving the cultural other is the primary expression of Jesus worship.

The Way of Jesus includes the daily practice of . . .

- loving people around us who are different from us.
- caring for people who may not speak our language.
- showing compassion toward people who hold a different nationality.
- learning from those around us who live in different communities.

Fundamental to following Jesus is showing love to people across cultural barriers. Neighbor love can look very different depending on what culture you come from. For some, caring for someone means showing up on time and leaving on time. For others, neighbor love means showing up late but sharing space deep into the night. In some cultures, neighbor love means reading between the lines to figure out what someone is really asking for. Conversely, in other cultures, friendship means asking very direct questions to gauge how to help. For some, neighbor love means spending lots of quality time together doing seemingly meaningless things. Others feel love by working together on a project or task. Some receive love by being helped, whereas others feel love by being empowered to help others. The list goes on and on!

Just as God expressed cultural humility by taking on a Jewish body, learning the Hebrew language, and dying on behalf of all peoples, followers of Jesus are called to express the same cultural humility in their daily lives. And from this foundation, we can learn additional lessons on cultural identity from other passages in the New Testament.

TAKEAWAYS

We express our love of God through our unique cultures.

The cultural Christ fulfilled the old covenant by ushering in a liberative stance on local culture. Jesus expects us to love God no matter what nation we live in. Jesus expects us to worship God regardless of our local traditions. Luke 10:25–28 teaches us to adore Christ by using our native language, with our unique food preparation, and in the normal way we exist culturally. Think of the ways you can love God in how you were created—not based on the expectations of other culture groups around you.

We express neighbor love by caring for the cultural other.

The cultural Christ expects all people to reach beyond their cultural identity to care for others. This is what God has done for us in Christ. Jesus reached down to human culture by taking on brown skin, eating kosher foods, and living within a marginalized community. Jesus did this to love us—the cultural outsider! This good news compels us to find ways to open our lives to the cultural outsiders around us. Think of those around you who are culturally different from you whom God is calling you to embrace.

Cultural humility is fundamental to the Way of Jesus.

The cultural Christ has taught us to foster a daily spirit of cultural humility. Followers of Jesus can't hold a spirit of arrogance or pride when it comes to culture. We must be willing to be wrong, to apologize, to ask questions, and to change our mind. Followers of Jesus must move from thinking that *culturally different is wrong* to thinking that *culturally different is a valid expression of God's image in the world*. The call in Luke 10:25–28 to love our neighbor must be understood through the lens of the parable of the good Samaritan—where neighbor love is a radical embrace of the cultural other.

CULTURAL FREEDOM IN CHRIST

Acts 10:9–28

Main point

▶ We are free to worship Jesus in our home culture.

In the early church, it was hard for Jewish Christians to imagine a faith where Jewish cultural practices were not mandatory to follow God. Up until Jesus, the concepts of culture, nationality, and faith were fully connected. For example, the old covenant taught that in order to become part of God's people, Gentile men had to be circumcised regardless of their ethnic background. Gentiles needed to adopt the Jewish cultural feasts, celebrations, and sacrifices outlined in the Law of Moses. Then, in the new covenant, Jesus declares that each person can express their faith regardless of the Jewish markers of language, ethnicity, or food laws. Where the old

covenant was culturally exclusive, the new covenant is marked
by cultural inclusion. In fact, one of Paul's primary reasons
for addressing local churches by writing letters was to correct
Jewish Christians who were expecting non-Jewish Christians
to act more culturally Jewish.

Even with this shift so deeply baked into Scripture, history
has shown that Western Christianity continues to suffer from
the same cultural elitism as the early Jewish Christians. Where
the early Jewish Christians often enforced Jewish ways of
living on Gentiles, Western Christians have enforced Anglo-
Saxon ways of living on non-Western people. This has been
especially true in the North American church.

THE COLONIAL CHRIST

John Eliot was a famous European missionary who came to
the British North American colonies on the wave of colonialism to evangelize Indigenous people in the New World. He
lived from 1604 to 1690 and spent much of his ministry in
the New England colonies. Eliot saw an opportunity to share
the gospel with the Native people in the region. Eliot came to
Boston "seeking the conversion of the [Native peoples]."[1]

While Eliot found it necessary to learn the local language
and live around the Indigenous population, he did not think
it was possible for Native people to follow Jesus in their local
culture. He created a separate European-based society for the
converts to live in, one in which the Native people had to abandon their language, dress, customs, and cultural expressions in
order to be Christian. Even after a person converted, Eliot was
known to withhold the sacraments of baptism and communion until the convert displayed a standard of "civilized" Western behavior. Only when Indigenous converts became *white*
enough did the missionaries allow them to fully participate in

baptism, communion, and church life. To be Christian was to become white. To be white was to be Christian.

It gets worse.

The Christian historian Ruth Tucker writes, "A biblical form of government, based on Jethro's plan in Exodus 18:21, was set up by Eliot; the town was divided into tens, fifties, and hundreds, each division with a ruling adult male. The white man's civilization became the standard, and Christian Indians were expected to simply accept it. To Eliot, true Christianity not only changed the heart and mind but also changed the lifestyle and culture. He could not envision a truly Christian community apart from European culture."[2]

Eliot and other European missionaries cast white people—themselves—as the "New Israel," inheriting the promised land of the Americas.

This exemplifies a massive historical problem that has plagued many Christians. Church history has taught us that Christians in charge have pretty much always mixed their cultural heritage with the Christian faith. Those in power often expect cultural minorities to adopt their language, customs, dress, nationality, or cultural values in order to follow Jesus. In this case, Christian maturity has less to do with following Jesus and more to do with assimilating to dominant culture. Though well intentioned, Eliot mapped the story of European conquest over top the story of the Scriptures.

While it may be easy for us to spot how other cultures have done this some four hundred years later, it's also easy for those inhabiting dominant culture spaces to ignore how this happens today. Because we each experience faith and worship from within our own unique cultural contexts, often surrounded by people who share this background, we may not even realize the ways that our understandings of culture and faith become intertwined. But there is good news: Jesus came to untangle this web of evil. Jesus came to set us free so that we can worship King Jesus from our unique cultural backgrounds. In his words and actions we find a powerful rejection of the colonial Christ that Eliot (and others) brought to the Americas.

ALL CULTURE IS CLEAN

Acts 10 is a pivotal chapter in the expansion of the early church. In Acts 1–9, Jewish Christians are preaching, praying, gathering, healing, and sharing with each other. Even Gentiles are deciding to follow Jesus! It was an exciting time. But the early church was also dealing with a big tension. The ethnically Jewish disciples of Jesus were asking, Do non-Jewish followers of Jesus need to give up their culture to be saved? Do Gentiles get to participate in church even if they do not celebrate our Jewish holidays and eat our food? Can you follow Jesus outside of the cultural traditions of Jesus? The Jews were also asking themselves, Does God want us to eat Gentile food? Is it okay for us to stop celebrating our Jewish holidays and hang out with Gentiles? These were really hard questions to answer. In response, God gave Peter a vision that changed the course of Christianity.

> About noon the next day, as they were on their journey and approaching the city, Peter went up on the roof to pray. He became hungry and wanted something to eat, and while it was being prepared he fell into a trance. He saw the heaven opened and something like a large sheet coming down, being lowered to the ground by its four corners. In it were all kinds of four-footed creatures and reptiles and birds of the air. Then he heard a voice saying, "Get up, Peter; kill and

eat." But Peter said, "By no means, Lord; for I have never eaten anything that is profane or unclean." (Acts 10:9–14)

For those who are accustomed to eating lots of different animals, this might not seem like a big deal. But it would have been engrained in Peter from a young age that only certain animals were clean to eat—that is, ceremonially pure and fit for food. Many animals were so unclean that ethnic Jews were not allowed to own them or touch them. Entire chapters from the Old Testament are dedicated to carefully mapping out which foods were okay to eat, and which were sinful to eat. Leviticus 11 and Deuteronomy 14 would have been ringing in Peter's mind as he watched this array of unclean animals get closer to him. *Pigs are off limits. Shrimp are wrong to eat. Eagles are sinful to digest. Rabbits are unclean.* Yet here was God telling Peter to *kill and eat.* Peter was learning that with the new covenant, God was allowing ethnic Jews to eat all food—and that was a big deal to an ethnically Jewish person who had been raised on these purity laws.

What was Peter's response to God's vision? Peter responded with the convictions of his Jewish upbringing. He replied in confusion: *No! What you have just told me to eat in this vision is unclean and blasphemous.* Peter understood these foods to be dirty and sacrilegious.

The voice said to him again, a second time, "What God has made clean, you must not call profane." This happened three times, and the thing was suddenly taken up to heaven. (vv. 15–16)

Right away, God corrected Peter—*Do not call these foods unclean. Do not call them profane. They are not dirty. They are not sinful.* God rebuked Peter's instinct to call the eating of these animals wrong. But the meaning of all this was still unclear to Peter.

Right after this vision, Peter went to Caesarea to meet with an Italian Gentile named Cornelius. Cornelius had gathered his family and close friends in his house to hear from Peter. Before the coming of Jesus with the new covenant, Peter would not have spent time eating and dining with Gentiles—remember, purity laws. Peter would have considered their language, their lifestyle, their table manners, and culture as dirty. But in this meeting, God gave Peter an opportunity to put into practice what he had learned in the vision.

Peter decided, in keeping with the Way of Jesus, to enter the home of a Gentile to spend time in the cultural setting of the other.

> And as [Peter] talked with [Cornelius], he went in and found that many had assembled, and he said to them, "You yourselves know that it is improper for a Jew to associate with or to visit an outsider, but God has shown me that I should not call anyone profane or unclean." (vv. 27–28)

Peter now fully understood. Through the vision, God had revealed that he should not consider any person from a non-Jewish culture unclean or dirty—not their cultural foods, table practices, or Gentile cultures. Peter was sitting in a house with people who spoke different languages, celebrated different holidays, raised their kids in a different way from the Jews, listened to different music, and came from different ethnic groups. On this day, Peter felt the freedom in Jesus to share space among these culturally diverse people for the very first time. He could eat what they served. He could share space in their home. He could engage with them without thinking their way of life was dirty or profane. Do you see the gap between the American missionary Eliot's approach and God's vision in Acts 10?

The implications of Acts 10 are far-reaching when considering cultural identity development. Consider the aspects of your culture that feel shameful or judged by others. Consider the parts of your body or cultural practices that you have been told are not good enough. God in Christ has given you a new teaching: Do not call a cultural expression unclean that God has called clean. Do not consider the lesser-known or shamed aspects of your cultural identity unclean or dirty.

According to Acts 10—
Your music is clean.
Your accent is clean.
Your family is clean.
Your language is clean.
Your eye color is clean.
Your skin color is clean.
Your face shape is clean.
Your nationhood is clean.
Your natural hair is clean.
Your favorite food is clean.
Your table practice is clean.
Your education level is clean.

Rich or poor—you are clean.
Single or married—you are worth it.
Citizen or refugee—you are esteemed.
Eastern or Western—you are unsoiled.
Boss or employee—you hold full value.
Young or old—you have cultural worth.
Homeless or housed—you are dignified.

What God has called clean, we must not call unclean.

Those who come from a majority culture are called to adopt the posture of Peter. This requires us to interrogate the ways we consider other cultural expressions unclean. The fatal flaw in majority culture spaces is that we treat our culture as cleaner and more holy than others. We pass judgment on cultural differences that are weird to us. Like the missionary John Eliot, we often expect people to accommodate our cultural perspective because we are the majority. We expect others to go with our cultural flow or get out of the way. Or worse, we tell people they must be like us to follow Jesus. This is what God is correcting in Acts 10! We are not more dignified. We are not more esteemed in the sight of God. We are not above embracing other cultural practices that God has given those made in God's image.

TAKEAWAYS

Jesus has made your culture clean.

God calls us to embrace aspects of our cultural identity that have been called unclean. Most people have aspects of their culture that they do not like or are slightly ashamed of. Perhaps it is the family you come from or the way you were raised. Your skin color, accent, education level, or where you live are all areas where you may have felt judgment. Many know what it feels like to be treated as unclean. Jesus came to embrace those aspects of your life. Jesus came to dignify and call clean what you struggle to believe is worth accepting. While the mirror in your room can speak lies over your body and culture, the mirror of God reflects the truths: beloved, beautiful, worthy, and clean like all others made in the image of God!

Jesus has made the culture of others clean.

Followers of Jesus must also look at those who are different as culturally clean. It is so easy to pass judgment on people who inhabit a different cultural space—judgments like, *Why do they eat like that? Why do they raise their kids like that? Why can't they be more civilized? Why don't they learn the language? Why are they coming here?* This passage should shape the heart of each Christian to walk into cultural spaces like Peter walked into the house of Cornelius. We must be open to the cultural other. We must embrace other cultural expressions as clean and dignified. Acts 10 moves followers of Jesus away from cultural exclusion to the posture of cultural embrace.

15

THE GOSPEL AND CULTURAL INCLUSIVITY

Galatians 2:11–14

Main point

▶ The gospel trains us to wisely steward our cultural power.

While Peter seemed to embrace Jesus' posture to dignify Gentile culture in Acts 10, a short time later he reverted to a posture of cultural exclusion in the city of Antioch. It was serious enough that Paul rebuked Peter in front of the church and included the story within a letter written to Galatia. Why was it so serious? According to Paul, Peter's cultural misstep meant that he was not living in line with the gospel.

THE CULTURAL IMPLICATIONS OF THE GOSPEL

In earlier chapters, we discussed that the good news of Jesus is given to people of all cultural groups who place their faith in the Jewish Messiah (Luke 4:18–21). The gospel of Jubilee, as we discussed in chapter 12, offers each of us an experience of vibrant spiritual life. But the gospel does not stop there.

While the gospel saves us, it also instructs us to live a certain way in the world. Put another way, the gospel is meant to save us and then teach us. This is the Way of Jesus. After accepting the good news of the gospel, we then grow into the gospel daily. Keep this principle in mind as we read about a very charged social situation that took place in Antioch.

THE GOSPEL AND CULTURAL DOMINATION

Antioch was the third largest city in the Roman Empire. It was very culturally diverse and was known to have ethnic strife among its people. A third of the city's population was enslaved and lacked the rights of ordinary Roman citizens. Paul had gone to Antioch to share the gospel to Gentiles, crossing cultures to make the gospel understandable to those who spoke a different language, had a different nationality, and had different daily customs. By the time that Galatians was written, the church comprised both Jewish and Gentile converts to Christianity. This meant that for the first time, these two groups were navigating how to fit together in community.

Our story picks up when the apostle Peter, also known as Cephas, visited the church in Antioch. Paul writes:

> When Cephas came to Antioch, I opposed him to his face because he stood self-condemned, for until certain people came from James, he used to eat with the gentiles. But after they came, he drew back and kept himself separate for fear of the circumcision faction. (Galatians 2:11–12)

In the early church, eating together was a central part of gathering. The church had a meal together and remembered the sacrifice of Christ by eating bread and drinking wine. This was often called the love feast. When Peter sat down to fellowship with Gentile Christians, as Paul tells us he did after he first arrived in Antioch, he was entering a new cultural space. He was sharing language, table manners, and customs with those who did not grow up like him. During the love feast at Antioch, cultural identities were blending in new ways to create a whole new kind of church—just as Jesus intended.

So what went wrong? We learn that after James and his crew showed up, Peter stopped spending time with Gentiles at church and began hanging out with the Jewish converts to Christianity. James was ethnically Jewish, just like Peter. Peter, James, and those with James would have spoken the same language, would have had a high level of cultural familiarity, and would have easily clicked together in conversation. They knew the same jokes. They knew the same songs. They ate the same way. They dressed similarly. Peter separated himself from the Gentile Christians because he cared more about what his own ethnic group thought of him.

I want us to consider the majority/minority dynamics in this church setting. Gentile Christians held far less cultural power than Jewish converts at this stage of church history. After all, they had not grown up in within Jewish culture. They had not walked with Jesus. They didn't know Hebrew and were not accustomed to the Jewish way of life. The Jewish Christians were the majority, the ones with a history as God's people, and the Gentile Christians were the minority group, the newcomers. With this in mind, how would the Gentile Christians have felt when Peter suddenly removed himself from fellowship? What would they have thought when Peter began displaying his faith in an exclusively Jewish way? What would Peter's actions have done to their understanding of

156 IN GOD'S GOOD IMAGE

Christianity? How would that have made them feel about the
way they spoke, ate, and acted in church?

Consider these questions as we continue with Galatians
2:13:

> And the other Jews joined him in this hypocrisy, so that
> even Barnabas was led astray by their hypocrisy.

Peter's decision to only spend time with his ethnic group in
church encouraged others to do the same. Christians in Antioch
began sorting along ethnic lines during the love feast. And as a
result, the Gentile converts began feeling pressure to act more
Jewish and abandon their cultural upbringings. Whether Peter
meant to or not, he instigated segregation at church. Paul notes
that even his disciple Barnabas was led in the wrong direction
by Peter. Paul uses the word *hypocrisy* twice in verse 13 to
communicate the double-mindedness of Peter and the others
who segregated themselves. Paul then writes:

> When I saw that they were not acting consistently with
> the truth of the gospel, I said to Cephas before them all,
> "If you, though a Jew, live like a gentile and not like a Jew,
> how can you compel the gentiles to live like Jews?" (2:14)

Paul made this cultural situation a gospel issue. Peter and
the other Jewish Christians who refused to intermix with Gentiles at church were not, according to Paul, acting in accordance with the gospel. How we steward our cultural power
matters. Our ability to be culturally inclusive is a gospel issue.
What could be more serious? Paul is teaching us that the issue
of cultural power, cultural inclusivity, and cultural care are a
necessary outworking of the gospel. These issues should be
addressed within the context of Christian community.

In the second part of verse 14, Paul asks a rhetorical question meant to expose the sin of the ethnic Jews in Antioch: *Why are you forcing the Gentiles to act Jewish when you don't even live like that anymore?* In Acts 10, we learned that God had set Jewish Christians free to eat whatever they want and speak whatever language they want. They were free of the Mosaic law. Yet when they followed Peter into a segregated Jewish cultural space at Antioch, it communicated to the Gentile Christians that they needed to be more Jewish—even as they themselves were free to release these purity laws.

When Peter and his Jewish friends began gathering separately at church, it caused the minority group of Gentiles to feel bad about their culture. They felt unclean. They felt compelled to live like ethnic Jews. They felt the cultural pressure to abandon the freedom they had in Jesus. This was not only wrong for Peter and his ethnically Jewish friends—it was not in step with the truth of the gospel.

For Paul, the gospel is a manifestation of cultural humility. The gospel compels followers of Jesus to become aware of their cultural blind spots and their cultural prejudices. The gospel challenges all of us, like Peter, to confront aspects of our cultural heritage that naturally exclude people and cause them to feel unclean around us. The gospel compels us to be mindful of how our cultural identity causes others to feel unclean or unworthy. The gospel teaches majority culture Christians that we must stay in line with the truth of the gospel in how we steward our cultural power.

TAKEAWAYS

Cultural inclusivity is a gospel issue.

We must consider the ways that our cultural identity can naturally exclude others in daily life. Developing cultural intelligence and an awareness of how you project in spaces around you is central to following Jesus. The gospel calls us to become aware of how our cultural identity can naturally exclude or include others. We must push into these areas of our life to create space for those who need the love of Jesus. When we manifest Christ's spirit of cultural inclusion, we are living in step with the truth of the gospel.

Cultural power should be acknowledged and stewarded.
It is critical for followers of Jesus to reflect on how their gender, class, family, ethnic background, race, class, and so on affect those around them. We are all located in a cultural space that holds power. That space comes with privileges that can be a blessing to others. Your cultural power can also harm people and cause them to feel unclean. This passage moves us beyond thinking about culture as neutral or unimportant. As followers of Jesus, we must understand and steward our cultural identity so others are loved and embraced and feel welcome in our presence.

16

DIGNITY FOR MINORITY IDENTITIES

Colossians 3:9–11

Main point

▶ God provides dignity and solidarity for those inhabiting marginalized identities.

Thus far in our biblical survey, we have not discussed the topic of race very much. This is because race did not function the same in biblical times as it does now. Why? While the Scriptures sometimes do comment on the color of someone's skin, ancient groups were not discriminated against on this basis. Yet in the current global context, race often plays a significant role in our cultural identities—both in how we understand our own and how we relate to others. In the modern era, the invention of race has had absolutely devastating cultural effects on people across the world. Race as a social construct was created to give access and privilege to some while justifying the mistreatment of millions of people based on skin color. These racial categorizations are wrong and evil. Race is one

159

of the only cultural identity markers that Scripture does not talk about at all. While those who lived in the ancient Near East were aware of skin color and sometimes remarked on it, this never grew into a system whereby entire groups of people were enslaved or harmed because of it.

So why bring race into the cultural identity discussion if the Scriptures do not directly address this cultural category? Just because something is extrabiblical or not mentioned in Scripture does not mean Christians should ignore it. There are many applications of the text that move beyond what is written. For example, the Bible does not speak to the issues of digital technology, modern weapons, or space travel. But those who follow Jesus should always be looking at ways to address modern issues with the ancient text of Scripture. This is especially true on any topic that causes human languishing or promotes the unjust treatment of people made in God's good image.

It's also important to acknowledge that during the colonial era, Christians played a massive role in creating the category of race in the first place.[1] They then used the concept of race to advance colonial goals. Today, many Christians deny the damaging effects of race and racialized colonization. Do you see the bait and switch? The current state of race relations is in part due to Christians, both those who created race during the colonial era and those who now deny its damaging effects! For these reasons, it is important to address race biblically and help untangle the damaging effects of this cultural marker from our cultural identities.

THE CULTURAL CATEGORY OF RACE

The modern concept of race first became an important part of human identity starting in the 1600s. As early Western scientists traveled the world and interacted with unfamiliar cultures, they began classifying people by their skin color, hair, and facial features. Over time, race became a social hierarchy, with white Europeans at the top. Early Western explorers thought those with darker skin were less civilized and displayed barbaric and subhuman tendencies. Conversely, these Western travelers thought that those with lighter skin color more closely modeled acceptable (read: Western) behavior.[2] Thus was born the social construct of race. This concept placed humans on a continuum between pale white and dark black. To be white meant you were purer, smarter, and entitled to access in society. To have dark skin meant that you were impure, less intelligent, and were open to many forms of mistreatment. European philosopher David Hume summarized the general conclusion of this era when he wrote, "I am apt to suspect the negroes in general and all species of men (for there are four or five different kinds) to be naturally inferior to the whites. There never was a civilized nation of any other complexion than white. . . . No ingenious manufactures amongst them, no arts, no sciences. On the other hand, the most rude and barbarous of the whites, such as the ancient Germans, the present Tartars have still something eminent about them."[3] Though race was never more than a *folk* science, the leaders in Europe cast these evil categories over the world through colonial expansion. Race then latched onto and grew within cultural identity.

Christians during this period found many ways to prop up race through misinterpretations of Scripture. For example, theologians looking to link racial categories to Christian belief took the curse of Ham (Genesis 9:18–27) to mean that God had cursed anyone with dark skin. This passage describes Noah cursing his son Ham's descendants (specifically Canaan) to be "servants of servants." Some interpreters, particularly during the transatlantic slave trade, falsely claimed that Ham's descendants were Black Africans and that the curse justified the enslavement and subjugation of African people. Other theologians would use the story of Babel (Genesis 11:1–9), where God confused the language of humanity and scattered people across the earth, to suggest that God intended for different races to remain separate and not intermingle. Worse still, Great Britain recast itself as the new Israel come to the New World of North America to conquer the Native peoples on behalf of God.[4] All of this laid the groundwork for European Christians to dehumanize non-white ethnic groups, violently conquer Indigenous peoples, and enslave Africans.[5]

In more recent times, race has been used to actively encourage segregation in churches, promote lynching and other acts of terror, pass the Chinese Exclusion Act, place Japanese Americans and immigrants in internment camps during World War II, and force Native Americans onto reservations. We have seen inequities in the treatment of people of color in the prison system and justice system. Are we beginning to see the problem?

Yet even amid the strong case for why race is ever-present in our culture and personhood, many are not aware of this aspect of identity or do not believe it should be talked about. But ignoring race is like ignoring a virus we created that now disproportionately affects a significant part of the population. Where it is easy for some to ignore race, for others it is impossible.

So how do we talk about an aspect of cultural identity that negatively affects people made in God's image? In the book of Colossians, Paul mentions several aspects of first-century cultural identity that were also never meant to be created. Like the cultural identity marker of race, the first-century categories of barbarian, Scythian, and slave were created to dehumanize and devalue people made in God's good image. Paul openly calls these out in his letter in order to challenge them. Colossians 3:9–10 is instructive for us as we consider how to understand marginalized cultural identities:

> Do not lie to one another, seeing that you have stripped off the old self with its practices and have clothed yourselves with the new self, which is being renewed in knowledge according to the image of its creator.

In this passage, Paul is in the middle of teaching followers of Jesus how to live in the world. He emphasizes that truth-telling is central to the new way of life that God desires for us. The act of shedding our old selves and embracing a new identity in Christ involves a commitment to honesty and integrity. Paul calls us to clothe ourselves with this new self, symbolizing a complete transformation in our behavior and attitudes.

At the end of verse 10, we learn that followers of Jesus are to tell the truth in order to reflect the image of their Creator. This renewal in knowledge according to the image of God is a continuous process, shaping us more and more into the likeness of Christ. In essence, every person in every culture is called to renew themselves after the Jewish Messiah who created them. This is the Way of Jesus. By telling the truth, we embody the character of Jesus and make his presence known in the world. Our commitment to truth from within our own cultural identity is a direct reflection of our commitment to Christ and his teachings. It is through this practice of truth-telling that we can truly live out our faith and demonstrate the transformative power of the gospel.

We continue in Colossians 3:11:

> In that renewal there is no longer Greek and Jew, circumcised and uncircumcised, barbarian, Scythian, enslaved and free, but Christ is all and in all!

Every person in every cultural grouping is taking part in the restoration that God offers in Christ. Paul says that there is "no longer Greek and Jew" at the beginning of verse 11. Paul is not saying it does not matter that people are in these cultural categories. Paul is also not trying to flatten cultural distinctions or to say that our cultural location is irrelevant. Rather, Paul highlights these cultural categories to emphasize the common renewal that all followers of Jesus experience. Let's explore each of the cultural identities highlighted in this verse—especially the marginalized cultural identities.

Greek and Jew are the two broadest cultural groups in the verse. To Paul's audience, to be Greek was to be privileged, to hold higher status, and to wield tremendous cultural power. Conversely, to be an ethnic Jew was to be part of a scattered ethnic minority that had undergone tremendous suffering in the region. Jews, in contrast to the conquering Greeks, were often oppressed and misunderstood by those in the Greco-Roman world. Those of Jewish ancestry would try to stay away from Greeks, and the Greeks would snub their nose at the Israelites. Before Jesus, these two groups wanted nothing to do with each other.

Paul also mentions the circumcised and uncircumcised. Anyone who grew up Jewish would recognize this distinction, because, as we have previously discussed, under the Mosaic law, following Yahweh required circumcision. Every Jewish boy had to be circumcised as a sign of covenant faithfulness. Circumcision was a major religious and ethnic divider between God's people and pagan outsiders. Paul's claim that both the circumcised and uncircumcised were undergoing the renewal found in Jesus was an extension of the radical teaching started with Jesus and continued by the apostles. God had opened the door for both groups to come together, united by common faith in Jesus. This should ask us to look at our own churches and faith communities and consider the ways that cultural expressions can divide us when God desires us to remain who we are in Christ while uniting behind him.

Paul next highlights the cultural identity of barbarians. The elite class of Romans called anyone who did not speak Greek a barbarian. This term was derogatory. It was insulting. It was ethnocentric. The cultural descriptor of barbarian was not at all something that dignified people made in the image of God. To be a barbarian was to receive a low social status that God never intended for anyone made in the image of God. Paul calls this title out in the list of people being renewed after the image of God in Christ. Paul is moving those who are called barbarian from a disregarded cultural identity to dignified cultural identity. This was a radical reordering of how Christians should treat fellow followers of Jesus and those outside the church.

Paul also highlights the Scythian people. The Scythians were a group of ancient nomadic people, originally from Central Asia, who were known for their skill in horsemanship and warfare. This cultural group was considered by many to be the most barbaric, uncivilized, and hostile people to Roman civilization. They were despised by the Romans because of their violent resistance to colonization. They fought hard not to assimilate to Greco-Roman culture. For their fierce cultural resistance, the very name Scythian was synonymous with uncivilized and violent. They were considered subhuman and anti-Greek. This was not only a marginalized cultural grouping—they were hated and hunted by the Romans. Paul intentionally calls out this class of people as those in the family of God, those welcome in the church of God, and those receiving dignity through the renewal happening in Christ. The mention of Scythians alongside Greeks, Jews, barbarians, and enslaved underscores the radical nature of the gospel's inclusivity. Paul is making it clear that the transformative power of Christ's redemption is available to all, regardless of their cultural background or social status.

Finally, Paul calls to our attention two broad cultural groups: enslaved and free. While there were many types of slaves in the Roman Empire, all had very little social access. Men were overworked. Women were incredibly vulnerable. Most enslaved people had few if any rights. Slaves could be bought and sold multiple times over the course of their lives. While those who were free in Rome did not all enjoy the status of citizens, it was still far better to be free. Enslaved people formed a broad cultural grouping that was also very marginalized. Paul draws attention to this social dichotomy to bring equality and dignity between those who were free and those who were enslaved. The opposites are brought to the same dignity rooted in the imago Dei. All were made in God's good image.

CHRIST IN ALL

At the end of verse 11, Paul argues that even amid these cultural differences, many of which dehumanize and devalue people, Christ "is all and in all." What does it mean for Christ to be "all in all"? It means that all these cultural groups have been made in the image of the same God. Where Rome placed people on a sliding scale, from esteemed Greek to subhuman Scythians, God dignified all cultural groupings alike. It also means that all groups are being renewed equally in the image of our creator Christ. These followers of Jesus experienced renewal from within their cultural locations. This is profound! Those rejected by the Romans were especially accepted by Jesus. Those who suffered under the weight of evil cultural designations were comforted by Jesus. Jesus models the dignifying process by talking to a Samaritan woman (John 4:4–26), by inviting himself to the home of a tax collector (Matthew 9:9–13), by letting the little children run to him (Matthew 19:13–14), and by prioritizing the place of tax collectors and prostitutes in the kingdom (Matthew 21:31). And it also means that Christ is drawing these different cultural groups into fellowship together. They are all brought into one spiritual family united under the cultural practices of baptism and communion. The dignity that Rome failed to show all is meant to be displayed by the church, as an embodiment of the countercultural love of Christ on earth. Colossians 3:9–11 teaches us to identify the cultural locations where people are suffering, to name them publicly, and to bring all into the warm cultural embrace of Christ.

Despite what the Roman Empire says,
all have been made in God's image.

Regardless of what American or any other culture teaches,
we all masterfully reflect the image of Christ.

Even amid sinister cultural categories like race,
all are valued under the doctrine of the imago Dei.

While the world says we do not belong together,
the cultural Christ was crucified to create a new community.

We all, equally, with beauty, creativity, and love, are
being renewed after the image of our creator Christ.

How does all this help us reflect on our current understanding and experience of the cultural category of race? First, it is important to note that the apostle Paul did not act like such social categories do not exist. Even though distinctions like barbarian or Scythian had no foundation in biblical truth, Paul applied the truths of the gospel for those suffering under the weight of dehumanizing social categories. Paul named these for the church, forcing them to face the categories that governed their daily lives. He called out existing hypocrisy and sinfulness that was hurting people. He named the ways that people are robbed of dignity in order to validate their experiences of hurt.

Paul also called out these categories to emphasize that we are all equally made in God's good image. Where Rome's social hierarchy existed to protect the powerful, the gospel of Jesus existed to renew everyone, especially those with little social access, in the image of Christ. God calls all people, especially the hurting, into the equal renewal found in Christ. Paul exposed the darkness of Rome to let the light of Christ bring dignity to all who are made in God's image.

Even though race is a human-constructed category, we cannot escape the fact that it has shaped all of our cultural identities and been the source of great suffering in the world. The Scriptures call us to address the social evils that exist around us. Naming racism as the persistent blight it has been on our world is just the start. Whether light-skinned, dark-skinned, or something in between, we must fight against all forms of ethnocentrism. Churches can do this by reviewing their policies, lamenting with those who come from ethnic groups who have historically suffered, and highlighting stories on Sunday that draw us toward deeper compassion and humility. We can also create programs where those who suffer racially are supported by the family of faith. All these ideas spring from the truth that we are all equally worthy of the divine protections afforded us by the imago Dei. Colossians 3:9–11 draws us back to the foundational truth that Christ is in all—especially in those suffering from marginalized cultural identities.

TAKEAWAYS

The Way of Jesus offers dignity to those dehumanized by society.

Scripture openly calls out and rejects cultural categories that devalue those made in God's image. We must identify the ways that our own family, our cultural group, or broader society treats people as lesser than others. Jesus followers are called to identify and speak out against the ways that groups of people have been devalued, including the treatment of lower economic classes, the cutting off of certain neighborhoods from public access, the creation of caste systems, such as in India, and the rise and abuse of race as a social category. We should be looking for ways to dignify and empower cultural groups that have been harmed in society.

The Way of Jesus leads us to rejects cultural categories that devalue those made in God's image.

The Bible explicitly condemns systems and structures that devalue human beings. For instance, James 2:1–4 warns against showing favoritism, and Galatians 3:28 declares that in Christ, there is neither Jew nor Greek, slave nor free, male nor female. These scriptures challenge us to examine our own prejudices and societal norms that devalue others. By recognizing and speaking out against such injustices, we align ourselves with the biblical mandate to honor the image of God in every person. This includes advocating for the rights of the economically disadvantaged, opposing the exclusion of communities from public services, challenging caste systems, and addressing the social construction of race.

The Way of Jesus calls us to a collective renewal after the image of our Creator.

The transformative power of the gospel is not limited to individual renewal but extends to the collective renewal of communities and societies. In recognizing the image of God in every person, we are called to work together toward cultural renewal. This means collaborating across cultural and social boundaries to bring about justice, peace, and reconciliation. By seeing each person as a reflection of God's image, we can engage in meaningful dialogue and cooperative efforts that lead to holistic renewal and the flourishing of all people.

A CULTURAL TAPESTRY FOR JESUS

Revelation 7:9–10

Main point

▶ All cultural identities find their purpose and resolve in Jesus Christ.

From Genesis to Revelation, the gravitational pull of Scripture is toward Jesus. All passages and prophets point toward Jesus. All things have been created by and for him. No matter where we were born or what culture we have grown up within, our cultural identity is meant to express the image of Christ. When we seek Jesus as the foundation of our identity, we are free to worship Jesus and reflect God's good image in the world. This is what it means to embrace a sacred cultural identity. We have learned that when we embrace a sacred outlook on identity, one that encompasses both our specific cultural locations and the many expressions of culture that fill our earth, we will worship Jesus and love our neighbor more effectively. The Bible teaches that the origins, aim, purpose, and destination of all culture are found in Jesus Christ.

THE LONG ROAD HOME

My wife and I love taking road trips with our kids. Since they were young, we have taken them on twelve-plus-hour trips, from LA to Seattle, Seattle to Idaho, Illinois to Rhode Island, and South Carolina to Indiana. Though we are now road trip pros, we didn't start out that way. Among others, there is one key we have learned to road trip success: we help our kids set healthy expectations. We tell them where we are headed and describe what we will do upon arrival. We have this conversation when we get into the car and begin answering all the fun and silly questions they have about the destination. The hope of arrival helps with the difficult drive.

The Scriptures also paint a vibrant picture of where we are all headed. While the road to worshiping Jesus in person may be long, our destination can help us in our present struggles. We, like kids on a long road trip, need to know where we are going. We need to know the hope we have in Christ. This future hope found in Revelation reveals a time when we are free to express our cultural identity to a God who designed us. The aim and end of the Scriptures help us get through the often-painful present, through the long stretches when it feels like we may never arrive anywhere at all.

In Revelation, we find a picture of a reality where every person, every nation, every nationality, and every people group—from the east to the west, from north to south, from young to old, from wealthy to impoverished, and from disabled to able-bodied—are gathered to worship the cultural Christ.

ALL PEOPLES WORSHIPING JESUS

The apostle John wrote the book of Revelation from the island of Patmos to followers of Jesus who were suffering under the persecutions of the Roman Empire. John was sent to this small and rocky island in the Aegean Sea because he was a political and religious agitator. Patmos was a place where the government sent people whom they saw as troublemakers, including those who threatened the norms of the empire.

On this island, John saw many visions from Jesus. He was told to chronicle these visions, which he did in the book we now call Revelation. In chapter 7, John receives a vision bringing the scriptural story line of culture to its crescendo. Starting in Revelation 6, John watches as a series of seals are opened that hold messages revealed only by Jesus. In Revelation 7:9-10, a select number (representing a perfect number) of God's people are gathered before Jesus. Then the vision shifts to a multicultural gathering that echoes God's original designs from the earliest pages of Scripture.

> After this I looked, and there was a great multitude that no one could count, from every nation, from all tribes and peoples and languages, standing before the throne and before the Lamb, robed in white, with palm branches in their hands. (Revelation 7:9)

Here we see a vast, diverse group of people from every corner of the earth focused on the Lamb of God. These cultural groups are aiming their affections, thoughts, voices, and attention at the sacred Son of God. This verse highlights the three cultural distinctives of ethnicity, tribe, and language. In history, these cultural differences have been the cause of ethnic tension, war, violence, and unfounded judgment. But here the very aspects of culture that are proven to divide us are brought together in harmony. Like a conductor harmonizing the various instruments in an orchestra, God is seen bringing together every cultural identity into a song that Jesus has written into the world.

Those standing before Christ are robed in white. The color white here symbolizes the cultural unity found in Christ and the purity of those who trust in the gospel of Jesus. They are unified in him, yet it is clear from their bodies and their languages that they still retain the markers of their culture. Each person and each people have been made holy and pure from within their spoken language, their cultural values, and their cultural locations. God has saved and set each cultural people free to worship the Lamb from within their unique cultural vantage point. The palm branches they hold represent the victory and peace that God has brought through the gospel. In the Greco-Roman world, palm branches were often associated with victory in athletic competitions or military conquests. In the Jewish culture, palm branches were symbols of triumph and victory.[1] In John's vision, the palm branches mean that Jesus has overcome evil, banished injustice, and gathered every nation to himself.

This vision connects deeply to the Table of Nations in Genesis 10. If the Table of Nations sets the stage for understanding God's intent that humanity become diverse, the great multitude from Revelation 7 is the culmination of God's diverse design for every people. In Revelation 7 we do not see all people assimilate to one nation, one language, and one common culture—rather, we see an echo of the diversity found in Genesis 10.

In Revelation 7:9, the fulfillment of God's redemptive plan is depicted as encompassing all the diverse groups listed in

Genesis 10 and, more, as signifying that salvation through Jesus Christ is available to every nation and people, regardless of their genealogical or geographical origins. This multitude before the throne signifies the ultimate gathering of God's people from all the divisions and distinctions that have historically separated humanity. The people included in Revelation 7 includes you. It includes me. It includes anyone, regardless of their cultural identity, who places their faith in Jesus for the forgiveness of sins.

Revelation 7:9 stands as a powerful testament to the cultural inclusion that the gospel provides, bringing together the scattered nations of the world into a multicultural community before our creator God.

We now move to Revelation 7:10:

> They cried out in a loud voice, saying,
> > "Salvation belongs to our God who is seated on the throne and to the Lamb!"

This verse echoes the truth spread across the biblical narrative—God alone is our Savior. In the gospel narrative, God called Jesus to enter human culture as the Lamb of God. Jesus embodied a particular cultural time and place to lay down his life for every tribe, nation, and people of the world. The Lamb is our eternal sacrifice made to redeem our cultural spaces and places. The blood of the Lamb covers our sin and the sin of our people. Furthermore, Revelation 7:9–10 indicates that the Lamb can bring a diverse humanity together through the salvation that God has accomplished. The redemption we long for in our bodies, in our hearts, and in our minds is found in the Lamb. The salvation that God offers in Christ unlocks the meaning to our lives, our purpose, and our cultural identities.

TAKEAWAYS

Jesus provides ultimate meaning to your cultural identity.

The passage in Revelation reveals, in a final sense, the true purpose and aim of our cultural identity. The Scriptures reveal that all human culture was created for Jesus and by Jesus. Every person, regardless of cultural identity, is meant to search for cultural meaning in the person and work of Jesus. In other words, Jesus unlocks our cultural meaning. We find this by searching the Scriptures, learning about the life of Christ, and seeking meaning in the context of Christian community.

Jesus will unify every culture group in the world under his kingship.

In a world fractured by sin, every person longs for a path forward. We all long for a light that can lead our world in a better and more just cultural direction. In a world marked by cultural exclusion, genocide, war, and colonialism, the power of the gospel has brought about a movement where unity is possible. The picture we see in Revelation 7 offers inspiration and hope as we navigate our own cultural identity and the personal struggles around us.

Followers of Jesus must live into the cultural unity found in Christ.

As Christians, we look ahead toward and long for the unity expressed in Revelation 7. God is showing through this vision that unity and diversity are possible in Christ, that Jesus has the power to bring every people together in his name and under his rule. People who speak various languages and occupy different cultural groups are meant to live into this future as we relate to one another. From our personal friendships to our church community to our family relations, we are called to the cultural unity found only in Jesus.

Part IV

PRACTICAL
TAKEAWAYS

18

CULTURAL DISCOVERY PROCESS

In these final chapters, we move to integrate the scriptural lessons we've learned into our own cultural identity development. After learning about these beautiful lessons from Scripture, we must decide alongside Jesus how to apply them to our life. The goal, above all else, is to develop our sacred cultural identity in order to worship Jesus and love our neighbor. Let's begin our journey to integrate the Way of Jesus into our cultural identity development!

We will follow a four-step process by which we discover our cultural identity, identify areas where we want to develop our cultural identity, and consider how to integrate our cultural identity into the Way of Jesus. This personal discovery chapter reads more like a workbook—it includes questions, sections for writing, and prompts for contemplation and application.

STEP 1: CULTURAL NARRATIVE
Use the following prompts to write out your cultural narrative. As you begin, consider the ten aspects of cultural identity (ethnicity, age, language, nationality, race, gender, family,

work, politics, and class). How does each apply to your own experience? While you should review these aspects of your culture, it is not important to include all of them. Think about where your people have come from, what is important to your own story, and your family history. Then consider the present. Reflect on where you are now: where you live, what language or languages you speak, and how you view the world. Last, consider where you desire to go. What are your goals? What job, relationships, or identity markers do you hope to integrate into your identity?

Ten aspects of culture: Ethnicity, age, language, nationality, race, gender, family, work, politics, and class.

Where you come from (3–5 sentences):

Where you are (3–5 sentences):

Where you are going (3–5 sentences):

What are the top three aspects of cultural identity that inform your narrative?

How, if at all, did you consider the Way of Jesus when you were writing this out? Why do you think that was so?

When, if at all, did the gospel of Jesus begin to shape your own story? How did this take place?

STEP 2: CULTURE MATRIX

The next step is to put these aspects of cultural identity into the culture matrix. This tool will help us better understand the intersections within our cultural identity.

As a reminder, the ten aspects of identity that we are exploring are language, family, ethnicity, race, class, nationality, politics, sex and gender, age, and work.

Input these ten aspects of cultural identity based on their degree of importance in your cultural narrative. For example, if you mentioned your ethnic background or family multiple times, put it in one of the bigger sections. If you didn't mention your work or nationality, put those in the smallest sections.

Biggest:

1.

2.

Big:

3.

4.

Regular:

5.

6.

7.

8.

Small:

   9.

  10.

Cultural Identity Matrix
Fill in Matrix with ten aspects of your cultural identity below:

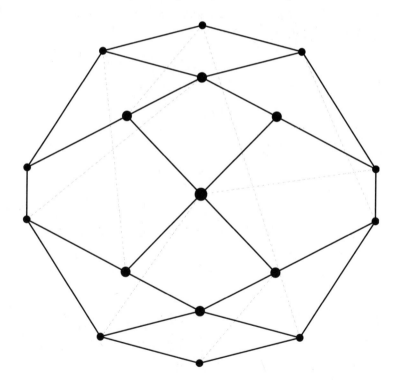

What have you learned by filling out the culture matrix?

Was it easy or difficult to assign relative importance to the ten aspects of cultural identity?

Are there any aspects of your cultural identity that you don't think about much?

STEP 3: PERSONAL INTEGRATION

Merging our cultural narrative and culture matrix

In this next step, we will combine our cultural narrative and culture matrix while considering what we have learned in this book. The takeaways from each passage covered in this book are listed later in this section for your review. While looking over these scriptures, read through and answer the integration questions. I encourage you to look back over the chapters in the event you need to reengage the specific passages in light of your own cultural identity.

How is your cultural narrative redeemed by the gospel of Jesus?

How do you see God's good image in your cultural matrix?

Where in the Scriptures does Jesus dignify your cultural identity?

Where in the Scriptures does Jesus affirm your cultural identity?

Where in the Scriptures does Jesus confront your cultural identity?

Key passages and takeaways

- *Genesis 1:26–28* Jesus dignifies human culture by creating all people in the image of God.
- *Genesis 10* Humans reflect the imago Dei by filling the world with cultural diversity.
- *Genesis 11:1–9* Humanity chose cultural uniformity in place of God's plan for cultural diversity.
- *Genesis 12:1–3* God created Israel to bless all cultures of the earth.
- *Deuteronomy 7:1–4* God used Israel to judge diverse cultural nations.
- *Daniel and Esther* The Israelites modeled cultural resistance while living as Jewish minorities in exile.
- *1 Kings 17:8–15; 2 Kings 5:1–14* The prophets give glimpses of the cultural dignity that Jesus will bring.
- *John 1:9–14* God is revealed as the Jewish Savior, born in a suffering cultural minority.
- *Luke 4:17–29* The gospel of Jesus Christ is meant for all cultures for all time.
- *Luke 10:25–28* Every person is called to love God and the cultural other.
- *Acts 10:9–28* We are free to worship Jesus in our home culture.
- *Galatians 2:11–14* The gospel trains us to wisely steward our cultural power.
- *Colossians 3:9–11* God provides dignity and solidarity for those inhabiting marginalized identities.
- *Revelation 7:9–10* All cultural identities find their final resolve in Jesus Christ.

STEP 4: PERSONAL ACTION PLAN

In this final step, we move from learning to reflecting to making concrete changes in our life. The following prompts can help you discern some possible next steps. It is critical to discern your own heart, life, and how you desire to love God and your neighbor more fully through your cultural identity. If this book is only an academic or intellectual exercise, we fail to follow the Way of Jesus. James 1:22–24 says:

> But be doers of the word, and not merely hearers who deceive themselves. For if any are hearers of the word and not doers, they are like those who look at themselves in a mirror; for they look at themselves and, on going away, immediately forget what they were like.

I encourage all of us to remember the words of Jesus' brother and move toward action!

I can love God with my cultural identity by doing the following:

I can embrace my neighbor with my full self by doing the following:

I want to serve Jesus through the use of my cultural identity in this way:

Jesus is calling me to develop _____ *aspect of my cultural identity:*

I have misused my cultural identity and need to confess the sin of:

I can embody the gospel of Jesus by displaying these aspects of my cultural identity:

Let's end with a prayer:

Dear King Jesus,
    May we display your good image in the world.
    Your great image of Peace.
    Your beautiful image of Love.
May we display our Creator—
    in the shade of our skin,
    on the land we reside,
    with the words of our tongue,
    to faithfully abide in your design.
Help us—
    follow you with our full selves.
    Embrace what you have made.
    Put on what you adore.
    To be more like you.
Amen.

19

GOD'S GOOD IMAGE FOR INDIVIDUALS

I'd like to share some simple takeaways for individuals look-ing to better display God's good image from their cultural location. These takeaways are meant to help each person walk in the Way of Jesus on a daily basis. Each takeaway encour-ages a deeper reflection on Scripture, a commitment to cultural humility, and a proactive approach to intercultural rela-tionships. By engaging in these practices, we can more fully embody the image of God in our diverse and interconnected world. Through self-reflection, hospitality, relationship-build-ing, inclusive practices, and humility, we align our lives with the teachings of Jesus, fostering communities that reflect God's love and justice. These principles guide us in transforming our cultural identities to better reflect the unity and diversity found in Christ.

SELF-REFLECT THROUGH SCRIPTURE

The sacred text of Scripture is the mirror by which we receive two things. First, we are to perceive the good image that God gave us. In this we are able to look at our bodies, minds, actions, and words and praise God for forming us in the image of our good God. We see that we are sacred and that we carry the divine footprint of God by virtue of the imago Dei. Second, the Scriptures reflect the Word, Jesus Christ, in our life. We are both affirmed and challenged by the Scriptures as they reflect back to us how we image God and, just as importantly, how we should image God in the world.

In the same way that Jesus called the two men on the road to Emmaus to understand all of Scripture through the lens of Jesus, we too must see our cultural identity through the lens of this work. If we want to reflect God's good image as individuals, we need to interrogate our own identity and cultural upbringing by allowing Jesus to dignify, shape, and confront all aspects of who we are. When we engage the Scriptures as the key to our cultural identity, we allow Jesus to make sacred our path toward cultural enlightenment.

Practically, this can be done by journaling responses to scriptural passages, engaging in community discussions that focus on diverse interpretations of Scripture, and applying biblical teachings to understand and resolve cultural conflicts. Embracing this perspective enables us to appreciate the imago Dei in ourselves and those around us, fostering a deeper respect for the diversity within God's creation.

In 1 Corinthians 12:12–14, Paul emphasizes the importance of diversity within the body of Christ: "For just as the body is one and has many members, and all the members of the body, though many, are one body, so it is with Christ. For in the one Spirit we were all baptized into one body—Jews or Greeks, slaves or free—and we were all made to drink of one Spirit. Indeed, the body does not consist of one member but of many." By understanding and integrating Scripture, we can more beautifully reflect the image of Christ in the world—cultivating a faith community that honors and celebrates cultural diversity, seeing it as a reflection of God's multifaceted image.

Reflection questions
- How does understanding that you are made in the image of God (imago Dei) affect how you view yourself and your actions?
- How can you practically integrate the teachings of Jesus into your daily interactions with people from different cultural backgrounds?
- What steps can you take to engage more deeply with the Scriptures to better understand your cultural identity in Christ?

DEVELOP CULTURAL HOSPITALITY

When I was planting a church in Los Angeles, an El Salvadoran family lived two blocks down the street from our family. In the neighborhood where we lived, there was a lot of historic underlying distrust between Mexican Americans and El Salvadoran Americans. In terms of population, the El Salvadoran community was outnumbered twenty to one. On our first New Year's there, this family made sure to invite my mixed-ethnicity family to their celebration event. We walked into a house packed with people from all over Los Angeles— music booming, drinks flowing, and a multigenerational buzz all around. Kids were spending time with their grandparents. Teenagers were talking with their *tias*. It felt especially sacred being invited into a family gathering of people who had just met us. The grandparents who owned the house came up to us with a full plate of food and a drink. In that moment, I thought to myself, "This minority family is expressing the cultural hospitality of God toward us!" They were embodying the kind of cultural hospitality that God was asking me to extend through our church planting efforts in the city.

The cultural hospitality that God showed us in Christ should shape our personal vision of intercultural hospitality. Furthermore, the greatest commandment to love God and our neighbor binds every follower of Jesus to a posture of cultural hospitality. Christians should foster a culturally hospitable spirit while speaking to others, eating with those who are different from them, and navigating new situations. The arms of Christ spread on the cross are our eternal reminder that God was killed to extend hospitality toward us. This sacrifice should shape our own daily sacrifice toward those God brings across our path.

To practice this, we can initiate meals or meetings in our homes or public spaces with people from different backgrounds, be intentionally inclusive in our language and actions, find ways to serve those around us who are dissimilar from us, and actively seek to understand rather than judge the cultural practices of others. As Paul writes in Romans 12:13, "Contribute to the needs of the saints; pursue hospitality to strangers." Additionally, Hebrews 13:2 reminds us, "Do not neglect to show hospitality to strangers, for by doing that some have entertained angels without knowing it." In Ephesians 2:14–19, Paul speaks of how Christ broke down the dividing wall of hostility, making peace between different peoples: "For he is our peace; in his flesh he has made both [groups] into one and has broken down the dividing wall, that is, the hostility between us. . . . So then you are no longer strangers and aliens, but you are fellow citizens with the saints and also members of the household of God."

By embodying this biblical mandate of hospitality, we live out the love of Christ and create a more inclusive and understanding community. This active effort to embrace cultural differences not only honors God's creation but also brings us closer to fulfilling the unity and love that Jesus envisioned for his followers.

Reflection questions

- How has God's example of cultural hospitality in Christ inspired you to extend hospitality to others in your daily life?
- What barriers or challenges do you face when trying to extend cultural hospitality, and how can you overcome them?
- How can you incorporate the practice of hospitality into your church or community activities to promote unity and understanding?

FOSTER MULTICULTURAL RELATIONSHIPS

One of the most transformative relationships I've ever had developed as I was learning under an African American pastor while church planting in Los Angeles. Pastor Martin is a musical artist, denominational leader, church planter, and corporate executive. He showed me what it meant to pastor, preach, and lead from a different cultural vantage point. It was through this, and other cross-cultural friendships, that I learned I inhabited social spaces that were particular to my people and ethnic group. I learned that my way of life was also different from that of many people around me. I learned that my own culture is specific and not general. While I would have acknowledged these truths cognitively, it did not become real until I was in relationship across the table with others who were unlike me. This kind of relational connection, fostered through time spent together, is central to living out the Christian faith.

The Gospels have many examples of Jesus crossing culture to share the love of God with the cultural other. Beyond the ministry of Jesus, the early church never would have grown unless Jewish converts were willing to learn a new language, go into new cultural spaces, and engage beyond their comfort zone. The gospel and the examples set by the apostles compel us to intercultural relationships. When we foster friendships beyond our own cultural identity, we grow in sympathy and empathy and will naturally be confronted with our blind spots and biases.

This can be practiced by participating in cultural exchange programs, volunteering in diverse communities, or joining multicultural groups and forums that allow for the sharing of different life experiences and perspectives. These actions will enrich our understanding and appreciation of God's diverse kingdom. By following these biblical examples and teachings, we can become more effective ambassadors of Christ's love, breaking down cultural barriers and building bridges of understanding and compassion. This commitment to intercultural relationships not only aligns with the teachings of Jesus and the apostles but also reflects the unity and diversity of God's kingdom.

Reflection questions
- How can you actively seek out and build relationships with individuals from diverse cultural backgrounds within your community?
- How has engaging in relationships with people from different cultural backgrounds transformed your understanding of your own cultural identity?
- What are some of the cultural biases or blind spots you have discovered through cross-cultural friendships, and how have you addressed them?

ADOPT JESUS' TABLE PRACTICES

When I was eighteen, I sat down with my grandfather Dale for a conversation that ended up shaping my understanding of the good image of God. We had just finished a Sunday lunch that my grandmother Jane had prepared. For three hours that day, I learned about Grandpa Dale's life growing up on the farm, living through the Great Depression, watching World War II unfold, and his conversion to Christianity after losing his first wife to suicide. We discussed how he moved from the racial prejudice of his college years to his first corporate job traveling around to African American schools to recruit students during the advent of affirmative action. Sitting across the lunch table, I was learning what it is like as a seventy-year-old who was also made in the good image of God. So much of this moment was made possible because of the rhythm of our families' table practice, where every week, we sat down for a meal. This conversation sprang up because we ate together, shared space together, and did not limit our interaction to a program or a set event. It happened in the rhythms of everyday life.

The Gospels show how Jesus displayed radical cultural inclusivity when it was time to gather with others over food. Jesus broke social and cultural norms by sharing meals with those on the fringes. He fed the multitudes, illustrating sweeping love that challenged the cultural elitism of his time. The Way of Jesus must include eating and spending time with those not typically included in the cultural norms of our daily life. The gospel paints a portrait of the nations being invited to the banquet table of salvation regardless of how broken or culturally different we are.

Jesus' interactions with tax collectors and sinners, such as in Luke 5:29–32, demonstrate this inclusivity: "Then Levi [a tax collector] gave a great banquet for him in his house, and there was a large crowd of tax collectors and others reclining at the table with them. The Pharisees and their scribes were complaining to his disciples, saying, 'Why do you eat and drink with tax collectors and sinners?' Jesus answered them, 'Those who are well have no need of a physician but those who are sick; I have not come to call the righteous but sinners to repentance.'" In Matthew 22:2–10, Jesus shares the parable of the wedding banquet, emphasizing inclusivity: "The kingdom of heaven may be compared to a king who gave a wedding banquet for his son. He sent his slaves to call those who had been invited to the wedding banquet, but they would not come. . . . Then he said to his slaves, 'The wedding is ready, but those invited were not worthy. Go therefore into the main streets, and invite everyone you find to the wedding banquet.' Those slaves went out into the streets and gathered all whom they found, both good and bad, so the wedding hall was filled with guests."

Adopting these practices might look like organizing community meals that are open to all, especially focusing on those who might feel marginalized or excluded. Encourage diverse food selections that honor different cultures, and create spaces where people feel safe to share their stories and experiences. By embracing these scriptural teachings and incorporating them into our daily lives, we can foster a community that reflects the inclusive love of Christ. Creating inclusive spaces where everyone feels welcome and valued at the table can transform our interactions and deepen our connections, mirroring the heavenly banquet where all are invited.

Reflection questions
- How can sharing meals with people from different cultural backgrounds enhance your understanding and appreciation of their experiences?

- What practical steps can you take to make your community meals more inclusive and welcoming of those who might feel marginalized or excluded?
- How can the practice of sharing meals together help break down social and cultural barriers within your church community?

CULTIVATE CULTURAL HUMILITY

It is hard to be humble. This is especially true in modern Western culture, which is one of outrage, self-righteousness, gossip, and political tribalism. The *right to be right* and *stating your point* are prized over *listening with both ears* and a posture of *willing to be wrong*. When was the last time you read through a social media interaction where someone said, "Wow, you are right and I am wrong . . . thanks for showing me!"? Yet 1 Peter 5:5–6 says, "And all of you must clothe yourselves with humility in your dealings with one another, for 'God opposes the proud but gives grace to the humble.' Humble yourselves, therefore, under the mighty hand of God."

Humility manifests in many ways. One of the most important forms of humility in a global era of diversity is cultural humility. This is especially true for Christians. Our biblical survey has shown that our attitude and daily life should be in keeping with the cultural humility that Jesus displayed when coming to earth. Followers of Jesus must encounter the cultural other as a teacher to learn from and must interrogate their own cultural values according to the life and teaching of Christ. Cultural humility is fundamental to faith.

Paul's words in Philippians 2:3–8 provide a profound model of humility: "Do nothing from selfish ambition or empty conceit, but in humility regard others as better than yourselves. Let each of you look not to your own interests but to the interests of others. Let the same mind be in you that was in Christ Jesus, who, though he existed in the form of God, did not regard equality with God as something to be grasped, but emptied himself, taking the form of a slave, assuming human likeness. And being found in appearance as a human, he humbled himself and became obedient to the point of death—even death on a cross."

To practice cultural humility, we must be willing to admit our limitations and biases, seek feedback from those of other cultures, and commit to ongoing learning about cultures different from our own. Engaging in dialogues about cultural experiences and systemic inequalities can also deepen our understanding and empathy. James 1:19 reminds us, "You must understand this, my beloved brothers and sisters: let everyone be quick to listen, slow to speak, slow to anger." By embracing cultural humility, we follow Jesus' example and teachings, fostering a spirit of learning, empathy, and respect. This commitment helps build a more inclusive and loving community that honors the diversity of God's creation.

Reflection questions
- What steps can you take to admit your cultural limitations and biases and seek feedback from those of other cultures?
- How does the example of Jesus' humility in Philippians 2 inspire you to approach cultural differences?
- How can cultural humility contribute to building a more inclusive and loving community in your church?

20

GOD'S GOOD IMAGE FOR CHURCHES

Christians are called to worship and live in community, so it is critical to reflect on how followers of Jesus reflect the image of God together. Throughout this book, we have seen how we can discover and find our cultural identity only in the context of community with God, nature, and those around us. We learn from Jesus that the central community upon which we diversely reflect God's good image in the world is the church. The church is where God's desire for cultural expression is most keenly seen and realized. By engaging with the church as a diverse and inclusive community, we embody the unity and diversity in the Way of Jesus.

This chapter outlines practical steps and reflections on how churches can better reflect God's image through diversity, cultural celebration, prioritizing minority perspectives, gathering through meals, engaging in community mercy, and normalizing cultural learning. These actions not only honor God's creation but also prepare us for the eternal, diverse community we will share in God's kingdom.

STRIVE TOWARD DIVERSITY

There is a lot of debate around whether churches should seek to be culturally diverse. Some pastors do not see cross-cultural engagement as an outworking of the gospel. But we know that a Christian church does not exist without a universal gospel, one that includes non-Jews into the salvation of God. The church would not have expanded into the Roman Empire without previously hostile Jewish converts breaking with their cultural traditions to learn new languages, go to new lands, eat new food, and learn to express their faith in a way where Gentiles can understand. In a pragmatically driven Western church, where it is easier to simply reach a small cultural subset, we have lost the nerve to strive toward diversity. We have forgotten that our faith is fundamentally cross-cultural in nature.

So many of the passages we surveyed point to the reality that God loves diversity, desires diversity, and wants people to embrace the cultural other. Churches should be on the forefront of displaying this diversity through inviting and welcoming minority attendees, developing membership pathways that are culturally inclusive, and empowering diverse community members into positions of leadership. Churches should take cues from the cross-cultural fervor of Paul's ministry, the diverse leadership in Antioch, and the diverse vision set forth by God in Revelation.

Acts 13:1–3 highlights the diverse leadership in Antioch: "Now in the church at Antioch there were prophets and teachers: Barnabas, Simeon who was called Niger, Lucius of Cyrene, Manaen a childhood friend of Herod the ruler, and Saul. While they were worshiping the Lord and fasting, the Holy Spirit said, 'Set apart for me Barnabas and Saul for the work to which I have called them.' Then after fasting and praying they laid their hands on them and sent them off."

In Romans 12:4–5, Paul emphasizes the unity and diversity within the body of Christ: "For as in one body we have many members and not all the members have the same function, so we, who are many, are one body in Christ, and individually we are members one of another."

To live this out practically, churches could implement targeted outreach programs that appeal to diverse community groups, establish multilingual services, celebrate multigenerational friendships, and intentionally recruit leadership that reflects the community's ethnic composition. As a general rule, churches should be just as, if not more, diverse than their surrounding community. From program to policies, churches should prioritize strategies geared toward seeing this biblical vision come true. If you live in a largely monoethnic area, you might seek out other forms of diversity, such as generational diversity or disability diversity. Or find ways to incorporate children into the highest levels of church life.

By actively pursuing and celebrating diversity, churches can embody the inclusive love of God, creating spaces where all people feel welcomed, valued, and empowered to serve. This commitment not only reflects the heart of the gospel but also prepares us for the eternal, diverse community we will share in God's kingdom.

Reflection questions
- How can your church actively pursue and celebrate diversity in its programs and regular rhythms?
- How can your church create membership pathways that are culturally inclusive and empower diverse community members?
- How can your church ensure that it is as diverse as, if not more diverse than, the surrounding community?

CELEBRATE CULTURAL DIFFERENCES

One practical way that churches can foster a spirit of cultural inclusion and humility is by celebrating cultural heritages during gatherings. Throughout this book, we have explored how God dignifies our cultures by making all people in the image and likeness of God. Churches have a massive opportunity to celebrate cultural differences in the foods they prepare, the cultural sensitivity they display in programming, and how they honor the unique stories of their people. Organizing cultural festivals, hosting themed Sundays that explore different cultures through music, dress, and liturgy, and inviting speakers from diverse backgrounds can enrich the congregation's understanding and appreciation of global Christianity.

During our church planting journey in Los Angeles, we often sought ways to celebrate the imago Dei in the various groups that attended our church. This often meant highlighting the stories of those from African American, Filipino, or Mexican American backgrounds. We harnessed the stories of leaders and parishioners in the church to celebrate the good work that God was doing in the lives of people who spoke different languages and lived in different parts of our city. When we celebrated these people, we sent a signal to the entire church that *you belong, you can be different, and we will celebrate the way in which God created you.*

By celebrating cultural heritages and fostering an environment of inclusion and respect, churches can reflect the diversity and unity of God's kingdom. This approach not only honors the unique contributions of different cultures but also builds a stronger, more empathetic community that values each member's background and experiences.

Reflection questions

- How can your church incorporate the celebration of cultural heritages into its regular gatherings and events?
- How can highlighting culturally diverse testimonies and stories enrich your congregation's understanding of global Christianity?
- What steps can your church take to ensure it honors and respects the unique stories of its members?

PRIVILEGE MINORITY PERSPECTIVES

This biblical survey has shown God's heart for those who have suffered and who have been culturally disempowered. The way of the world teaches churches to cater to the majority culture group and to high-net-worth individuals in churches. Yet Jesus' teachings consistently highlight God's care for the marginalized. In Matthew 25:35–36, Jesus says, "For I was hungry and you gave me food, I was thirsty and you gave me something to drink, I was a stranger and you welcomed me, I was naked and you gave me clothing, I was sick and you took care of me, I was in prison and you visited me." This passage underscores the importance of caring for those who are often overlooked by society. James 1:27 further emphasizes the call to support the marginalized: "Religion that is pure and undefiled before God the Father is this: to care for orphans and widows in their distress and to keep oneself unstained by the world." In Acts 6:1–7, the early church set an example by appointing deacons to ensure that the needs of the Hellenistic widows were met, demonstrating the importance of including and caring for minority groups within the church community.

Our scriptural survey should lead churches in the Way of Jesus, whereby we prioritize the needs of minorities in our churches. This could mean creating support programs for the very young, very old, immigrants, refugees, or those who have lost their jobs. Churches can create advisory boards that include minority group members to ensure their voices are not only heard but also have influence over church decisions. These biblical principles mean that we feature and hold up the stories of those who have not had a voice in our church or community. Contrary to worldly wisdom, we give the microphone to honor the voices of those who are not the majority in our church but who often hold the deepest wounds and longest journeys toward wholeness.

Reflection questions
- How does prioritizing minority perspectives align with Jesus' teachings and the early church's example?
- How can featuring and honoring the stories of marginalized individuals strengthen your church community?
- How can your church address the systemic issues affecting minority groups in your local context?

GATHER OVER MEALS

During a sermon, I once asked, "What is your most memorable moment with someone you love?" The church crowd of about fifty people began telling stories of times of laughter, tears, death, and amazing moments with those they loved—family, friends, and other loved ones. I then asked, "What is one fairly common thread throughout all these stories?" A woman in the back said, "Food! Most of the time people were out somewhere eating or at home with family." One of the most critical aspects of cultural identity not mentioned much in this book is the preparation, eating, and power of a meal. So many cross-cultural moments are made possible for churches when potluck replaces (or becomes!) the program.

The Gospels are replete with instances where Jesus gathers with people over food. From turning water into wine to eating with sinners to a final communion with his disciples, Jesus teaches us that faith is meant to be expressed around tables of food and fellowship. Churches should make every program and preaching event an opportunity for fostering life-on-life meals where culturally distant peoples can form bonds of friendship in community. Hosting regular community dinners, potlucks with a focus on sharing stories, or small group gatherings in homes are effective ways to build deeper cultural connections and learning.

John 2:1–11 describes Jesus' first miracle at a wedding in Cana, where he turned water into wine, highlighting the importance of celebration and community: "When the wine gave out, the mother of Jesus said to him, 'They have no wine.' And Jesus said to her, 'Woman, what concern is that to you and to me? My hour has not yet come.' . . . Jesus said to [the servants], 'Fill the jars with water.' And they filled them up to the brim. . . . [and the water] had become wine." Acts 2:46–47 describes the early church practice of gathering for meals: "Day by day, as they spent much time together in the temple, they broke bread at home and ate their food with glad and generous hearts, praising God and having the goodwill of all the people. And day by day the Lord added to their number those who were being saved."

By gathering through meals, churches can create welcoming spaces where individuals from diverse backgrounds can share their stories, build friendships, and deepen their faith. This practice not only follows the example of Jesus but also

fosters a sense of belonging and unity within the church community. It has been said that one has not shared their culture
with another until they share their food.

Reflection questions
- How does the practice of sharing meals reflect Jesus'
  example and teachings?
- How can community dinners and potlucks become
  opportunities for cultural exchange and understanding?
- What are some ways that your church could use meals
  to build bridges and deepen relationships within
  the community?

ENGAGE IN COMMUNITY MERCY

One of the strongest biblical strategies for cross-cultural
engagement is finding ways to spread mercy and justice
through church activity.

Luke 4:18–19 recounts Jesus' mission statement: "The
Spirit of the Lord is upon me, because he has anointed me
to bring good news to the poor. He has sent me to proclaim
release to the captives and recovery of sight to the blind, to
set free those who are oppressed, to proclaim the year of the
Lord's favor." The gospel that Jesus declares in Luke 4 provides a blueprint for embodying justice in the world. Churches
that are serious about cultural engagement must be sensitive
to the needs of cultural groups who are suffering injustice.
In the same way that Jesus was active in loving and support-
ing those around him who were suffering, churches must see
local mercy efforts among cultural groups who are suffering
as intrinsic to their call.

Micah 6:8 calls believers to act justly and love mercy: "He
has told you, O mortal, what is good, and what does the LORD

require of you but to do justice and to love kindness and to walk humbly with your God?" This could involve partnering with local charities, creating ministries aimed at addressing specific community issues such as homelessness or domestic violence, empowering those in the church to address these issues, and training congregants in compassionate outreach and advocacy. By engaging in community mercy, churches can live out the gospel message and make a tangible impact in their local context. This commitment to justice and mercy not only honors the teachings of Jesus but also builds bridges across cultural divides, fostering a more inclusive and compassionate community.

Reflection questions
- How does engaging in community mercy efforts foster a more inclusive and compassionate church environment?
- How can your church identify and address the specific needs of cultural groups suffering injustice locally?
- How can your church embody Jesus' mission to the gospel of Jubilee (Luke 4) in order to enhance intercultural community?

NORMALIZE CULTURAL LEARNING

This might seem obvious, but it's important for churches to embrace a posture of cultural learning as a community. While it is easier to apply individually, churches can find ways to normalize learning about others in the practices, programs, preaching, and ongoing ministries of church life.

Ephesians 4:3–6 emphasizes unity in diversity: "[Make] every effort to maintain the unity of the Spirit in the bond of peace: there is one body and one Spirit, just as you were called to the one hope of your calling, one Lord, one faith, one baptism, one God and Father of all, who is above all and through all and in all." One of the central ways that intercultural churches maintain the bond of peace is by normalizing listening to those who are different from you.

Churches should be spaces that talk about culture and push into Jesus-centered cultural development. This takes place when faith communities foster spaces where churchgoers can be open about their own cultural journeys, ask questions about those with whom they are in community, and reflect together on how Jesus helps us navigate cultural differences. Offering workshops, sermon series, and discussion groups focused on cultural intelligence and sensitivity can help educate and equip church members to engage more effectively with the world around them.

By normalizing cultural learning, churches can create environments where understanding and respect for diverse backgrounds are integral to spiritual growth. This commitment helps the church better reflect the inclusive and diverse nature of the body of Christ, fostering a community that is both welcoming and united in its mission.

Reflection questions
- How can your church create spaces for open dialogue about cultural journeys and experiences?
- How can workshops, sermon series, and discussion groups focused on cultural intelligence and sensitivity benefit your congregation? What might these topics look like?
- What resources and tools can your church use to enhance cultural learning and understanding among its members?

21

GOD'S GOOD IMAGE FOR PASTORS

Pastors and church leaders have an incredible responsibility to synthesize the lessons in the Scriptures as they relate to their own cultural identity and put them into concrete action steps in the context of a community. This chapter is designed to equip pastors with practical tools and reflections that will help them lead their congregations toward embodying God's good image more fully. While no church or community is the same, these broad takeaways can guide church leaders in the right direction. By integrating the principles of inclusivity, cultural sensitivity, and prophetic witness into their ministry, pastors can create vibrant, diverse, and compassionate communities of faith.

By emphasizing inclusivity, addressing power dynamics, engaging in diverse discipleship, and fostering intercultural dialogue, church leaders can help their congregations follow Jesus in a particular place and time. These steps not only honor God's creation but also prepare communities for the eternal, diverse fellowship that Revelation 7 is pointing toward.

PREACH THE UNIVERSAL GOSPEL

Pastors—it's important to proclaim the same radically inclusive gospel declaration found in Luke 4. Romans 10:12–13 states, "For there is no distinction between Jew and Greek; the same Lord is Lord of all and is generous to all who call on him. For 'everyone who calls on the name of the Lord shall be saved.'" Acts 10:34–35 recounts Peter's revelation about God's impartiality: "I truly understand that God shows no partiality, but in every people anyone who fears him and practices righteousness is acceptable to him."

Consider how to teach the gospel through the lens of the cultural inclusion of Gentiles, foreigners, and those who are not from a Jewish background. When pastors emphasize the inclusion of all people into God's plan, they lay a foundation for cultural sensitivity, humility, and a willingness to engage like Jesus across cultures. Practical steps include using diverse examples and stories in sermons that reflect the community's multicultural makeup and regularly highlighting scriptural passages that discuss inclusion and acceptance, thus preparing the congregation to embrace a broader, more inclusive view of the kingdom of God. The gospel should be read as radically as it was understood in the first century.

By embracing these principles, pastors can help their congregations understand that the gospel's inclusivity is central to its message. This understanding encourages believers to engage with people from all cultural backgrounds, reflecting the diverse and unified body of Christ. The radical inclusivity of the gospel, when taught and practiced, transforms the church into a community that mirrors the kingdom of God, welcoming all and celebrating the richness of diversity.

Reflection questions

- How can you emphasize the inclusivity of the gospel in your teaching to ensure all feel welcomed and valued?
- What strategies can you employ to help your congregation understand and embrace a broader, more inclusive view of the kingdom of God?
- What steps can you take to ensure that your preaching remains as radically welcoming as it was in the first century?

DRAW OUT CULTURAL NUANCE IN BIBLE INTERPRETATION

I had just finished a sermon on the parable of the good Samaritan at a church retreat when a Chinese American woman came up to me and said, "I never heard that story explained like that before." When I asked what she meant, she explained that although she had been going to a church for fifteen years, she didn't know about Jesus' cultural background or social context or what was at stake for him as he told that story to the crowd. She began relating it to her cultural situation and the honor/shame dynamics valued by her family. Then she thanked me for unpacking the passage in this way. But I didn't do anything special! What I can do, and did do, was commit to helping all of us get into the cultural background and history of the Bible to show how we can humbly understand the text. The original culture matters. The social backgrounds are deeply important to the text.

It's important for pastors and leaders to elucidate the sociocultural realities of Scripture when teaching, preaching, or leading Bible studies. Exploring cultural nuances within the text helps congregants appreciate the cultural gaps between the text and those learning in church. It also helps readers self-assess their own cultural perspectives alongside the cultural backgrounds of the text they are studying. Leaders can enhance their teachings by using biblical background resources to provide a richer, more informed context for scripture interpretation. By integrating these cultural insights into their applications, leaders help their congregation bridge the gap between ancient texts and modern-day cultural contexts. This approach not only deepens understanding but also enriches the application of biblical principles in diverse cultural settings.

By providing cultural and historical context in their teachings, leaders help their congregants not only understand the text more deeply but also see the relevance of biblical principles in their own cultural contexts. This method of teaching fosters a more inclusive and comprehensive understanding of Scripture, encouraging believers to live out their faith with greater empathy and cultural awareness.

Reflection questions
- How are you communicating the sociohistorical nuance of biblical passages to help your congregation grow in cultural humility and learning?
- How are you bridging the Middle Eastern honor/shame context of the Scriptures with the cultural context in which you teach?
- How can you encourage your congregants to self-assess their own cultural perspectives alongside the cultural backgrounds of the Bible?

DEVELOP A PROPHETIC WITNESS

It is critical for church pastors and leaders to press into areas of cultural injustice by modeling their ministries after Jesus, who was willing to side with those who suffer. Jesus aligned with the prophets of the Old Testament, who were willing to speak hard truths to power, even at great personal risk. In Isaiah 1:17, the call to justice is clear: "Learn to do good; seek justice; rescue the oppressed; defend the orphan; plead for the widow." Jesus exemplified this prophetic witness in Luke 4:18–19 when he declared his mission: "The Spirit of the Lord is upon me, because he has anointed me to bring good news to the poor. He has sent me to proclaim release to the captives and recovery of sight to the blind, to set free those who are oppressed, to proclaim the year of the Lord's favor." Furthermore, in Matthew 23:23, Jesus criticizes the religious leaders for neglecting justice and mercy: "Woe to you, scribes and Pharisees, hypocrites! For you tithe mint, dill, and cumin, and have neglected the weightier matters of the law: justice and mercy and faith. It is these you ought to have practiced without neglecting the others."

Pastors must develop their prophetic leadership in tandem with pastoral care. While one can never be sacrificed for the other, speaking truth to power, entering prophetic lament, and addressing cultural blind spots should be central to the role of church leaders. Leaders can engage in community issues through public forums, writing articles that challenge societal norms and injustices, or participating in community demonstrations that align with the Way of Jesus. Additionally, creating sermon series that address current cultural issues, providing biblical perspectives on these issues, and facilitating workshops that equip the congregation to understand and act on these matters can reinforce a church's commitment to prophetic witness.

By embracing a prophetic witness, church leaders can inspire their congregations to take a stand against injustice and work toward a more equitable and compassionate society.

This approach not only honors the legacy of Jesus and the prophets but also demonstrates the church's commitment to living out the gospel in tangible and transformative ways.

Reflection questions

- How can you model your ministry after Jesus by addressing areas of cultural injustice?
- What practical steps can you take to develop your prophetic leadership alongside your pastoral care?
- What benefits do you see in fostering a church community that actively works toward a more equitable and compassionate society?

ADDRESS POWER DYNAMICS

The gospel guides leaders to address power dynamics within their congregations and leadership teams. The disagreements between Peter and Paul, as illustrated in Galatians 2 (see Chapter 15 of this book), serve as a timeless lesson on the importance of confronting and resolving internal conflicts. Beyond the example of Paul rebuking Peter in Antioch, James 2:1–4 warns against favoritism and partiality: "My brothers and sisters, do not claim the faith of our Lord Jesus Christ of glory while showing partiality. For if a person with gold rings and in fine clothes comes into your assembly, and if a poor person in dirty clothes also comes in, and if you take notice of the one wearing the fine clothes and say, 'Have a seat here in a good place, please,' while to the one who is poor you say, 'Stand there,' or, 'Sit by my footstool,' have you not made distinctions among yourselves and become judges with evil thoughts?" Moreover, Isaiah 58:6–7 emphasizes the call to address systemic injustice: "Is not this the fast that I choose: to loose the bonds of injustice, to undo the straps of the yoke, to let the oppressed go free, and to break every yoke? Is it not to share your bread with the hungry and bring the homeless poor into your house; when you see the naked, to cover them and not to hide yourself from your own kin?"

Leaders should foster open dialogue about power dynamics, implement church structures that promote equality, and transparently acknowledge and rectify their failures. Regular training sessions on power and privilege, as well as facilitated discussions on these topics, can help create a more equitable and just community.

Practically, this means speaking openly about topics of race, social disparity, poverty, and community issues that disproportionally affect those without political or social access. The church must be the city on a hill that deals with these issues in keeping with the Way of Jesus. By addressing power dynamics and fostering an environment of transparency and equality, church leaders can create a community that truly reflects the inclusive and just nature of the gospel. This approach not only helps build trust and unity within the church but also demonstrates to the wider world the transformative power of living out the teachings of Jesus.

Reflection questions

- What does it tangibly look like to keep in step with the truth of the gospel as it relates to power, cultural empowerment, and issues faced in Galatians 2?
- How can you foster open dialogue about power dynamics within your congregation and leadership team?
- What steps can you take to implement church structures that promote equality and address power imbalances?

SUBMIT TO DIVERSE DISCIPLESHIP

It is vital for pastors and leadership teams to engage in discipleship with mentors from culturally diverse backgrounds. This practice not only models the cultural humility expected of their congregants but also enriches leaders' perspectives and enhances their approach to ministry. Paul's relationship with Timothy, who had a Greek father and a Jewish mother, is an example of cross-cultural discipleship (Acts 16:1–3). This mentorship allowed both men to grow in their understanding and ministry. Acts 18:24–26 highlights the role of Priscilla and Aquila, a Jewish couple, in mentoring Apollos, an eloquent speaker from Alexandria: "Now there came to Ephesus a Jew named Apollos, a native of Alexandria. He was an eloquent man, well-versed in the scriptures. . . . When Priscilla and Aquila heard him, they took him aside and explained the Way of God to him more accurately."

Church leaders who are serious about intercultural ministry must seek out and participate in cross-cultural mentorship through diverse theological learning, by learning from the global Christian community, and by developing intercultural competencies that affect their daily leadership. Churches can also create pathways for non-majority culture churchgoers to enter into positions of leadership regardless of education level or language spoken. This commitment shows the congregation the value of learning from diverse voices and experiences.

By submitting to diverse discipleship, pastors and leaders demonstrate their commitment to cultural humility and the value of diverse perspectives in the body of Christ. This practice enriches their leadership and sets a powerful example for their congregation, fostering a more inclusive and understanding church community. This commitment to learning from diverse voices aligns with the biblical vision of unity and diversity within the church, as seen in passages like Revelation 7:9–10, where a multitude from every nation, tribe, people, and language worships together before the throne of God.

Reflection questions
- What lessons can be learned from biblical examples of cross-cultural discipleship, like Paul and Timothy or Priscilla and Aquila with Apollos?
- What steps can you take to seek out cross-cultural mentorship and diverse theological learning?
- How can creating pathways for non-majority culture churchgoers to enter leadership roles influence your church community?

FOSTER INTERCULTURAL DIALOGUE
Creating spaces for intercultural dialogue within the church community is essential. Romans 12:10 encourages believers to "love one another with mutual affection; outdo one another in showing honor." This command was written to a culturally diverse church in Rome and underscores the importance of valuing and respecting each other's cultural backgrounds. Acts 2:5–11 depicts the day of Pentecost, where people from various nations heard the gospel in their own languages: "There were devout Jews from every people under heaven living in Jerusalem. And at this sound [of many spoken languages] the crowd gathered and was bewildered, because each one heard them speaking in the native language of each. Amazed and astonished, they asked, 'Are not all these who are speaking Galileans? And how is it that we hear, each of us, in our own native language?'"

Pastors and leaders can initiate this by organizing events and programs that celebrate different cultures, such as international food fairs, integrating multiple languages into the liturgy, and highlighting culturally diverse testimonies. Facilitating small group discussions that focus on cultural experiences or book studies on global Christianity can also promote understanding and empathy. These activities not only celebrate diversity but also help majority community members understand and appreciate the perspectives and challenges of minority groups, leading to a more inclusive and empathetic church environment.

By fostering intercultural dialogue, church leaders can create an environment where all members feel valued and understood. This practice not only enriches the spiritual life of the community but also reflects the inclusive and diverse nature of God's kingdom. Engaging in these dialogues helps build bridges between different cultural groups, promoting peace, unity, and mutual respect within the church.

Reflection questions
- What practical changes can you make to increase cultural learning and dialogue in your church?
- How can you incorporate intercultural dialogue and learning into your Sunday service?
- How can small group discussions focused on cultural experiences or book studies on global Christianity promote empathy and understanding?

Appendix

THE CULTURE SPECTRUM

Main point

▶ Individuals hold many cultural values based on their cultural upbringing.

The culture spectrum explores our natural cultural disposition toward a range of issues. This tool helps us understand the massive influence of our native culture on eight key issues. For those who want to dive deeper into cultural understanding, intelligence, and identity, this is a great place to start. The spectrum helps individuals recognize their position within these eight areas by looking at other ways of expressing culture in the same situation. If used properly, this tool is meant to increase your personal cultural awareness and identify the ways we judge others who do not hold the same value.

There are eight sections to the spectrum: ethics, group interaction, work and relationships, communication, gathering, celebration, age, and money. Within each of these areas, you might hold one of two opposite values. To use celebration as an example, some people in the world learn from a young age to extend respect by showing up at the exact time an event is said to start. It can be disrespectful to show up late or stay later than the designated time. Some feel the cultural pressure to apologize for showing up late based on the cultural value of *timeliness*. Other cultures are not concerned with showing up on time but instead are driven by the relational connectivity of the event. In this case, respect has nothing to do with showing up or leaving on time. Rather, it can be offensive to leave in the middle of a daylong celebration. We are all taught from a young age, usually without an explicit lesson, how we are to relate to community events and celebration.

Many people hold these cultural values without even thinking about it. These values are often unconscious convictions that come out only when they are challenged. Someone can live their whole life and never think about where they fall on issues of conflict, celebration, or work conduct. This is especially true if someone lives in the same cultural community most of their lives.

Cultural values are often exposed when we engage cross-culturally. These differences can cause a range of negative responses, including confusion, anger, disengagement from the situation, or judgment. When exposed to a different cultural value for the first time, it can be hard to accept the difference as equally valid. In the culture spectrum chart on pages 227–229, the comments set in parentheses are meant to reveal the common judgments we can have. For example, indirect communication can seem disingenuous or dishonest if you are not used to this cultural value. On the other side, direct communication can seem aggressive or hostile if you have not been exposed to this cultural value. The phrases in parentheses are meant to help you identify common judgments to avoid. Ideally, cross-cultural interactions can also cause the positive responses of discussion, curiosity, cultural humility, or self-reflection. This book shows us how the Way of Jesus leads us toward acceptance and humility and away from bias or cultural pride toward others.

CULTURAL CATEGORIES

The eight cultural categories are meant to help you think about your own position on the spectrum. While the spectrum presents cultural differences in a binary way, the truth for you could be somewhere in between. I suggest that you identify where you fall on these continuums by ranking yourself somewhere between the two ends of the spectrum.[1] I have provided five points between each side to measure where you fall on the spectrum. The left side of this continuum more closely resembles Eastern cultures; the right side better represents Western cultures. Of course, many culture groups and regions of the world do not fit neatly into one position or another.

Ethics

Shame-based: Influenced by societal norms and fear of misrepresenting the community.	**Guilt-based:** Guided by personal conscience and internal sense of right and wrong.
Social respect: Aimed at maintaining communal harmony and collective well-being.	**Personal conscience:** Driven by individual moral judgment and self-reflection.

Group interaction

Social harmony: Prioritizing group cohesion and consensus in interactions.	**Personal freedom:** Emphasizing individual choice and autonomy in opinions/perspectives.
Community-oriented: Valuing collective identity and mutual support.	**Individual-oriented:** Prioritizing personal goals and self-expression.

Work and relationships

Hierarchy in relationships: Basing interactions on established ranks and authority levels.	**Equality in relationships:** Treating everyone as equal, regardless of status or role.
Relational approach: Focusing on building and maintaining interpersonal connections.	**Results-oriented approach:** Prioritizing efficiency and outcomes in tasks and interactions.

Communication

Indirect communication: Conveying messages subtly to avoid confrontation.	**Direct communication:** Expressing thoughts and intentions frankly to get point across.
Conflict avoidant: Steering clear of confrontations to maintain peace and harmony.	**Assertive engagement:** Addressing disputes directly to resolve issues.

Gathering

Event-oriented gathering: Focusing on the experience and people of social events to honor those involved.	**Time-oriented gathering:** Value punctuality, schedules, and efficiency in social events to respect those involved.

Celebration

Expressive celebration: Demonstrating joy and happiness openly and loudly.	**Quiet celebration:** Marking joyous occasions in a subdued, calm manner.

Age

Value elders: Emphasizing respect and reverence for older individuals.	**Value youth:** Focusing on the ideas, preferences, and contributions of younger people.

Money

Financial patronage: Relying on and contributing to a network of financial interdependence.	**Financial independence:** Prioritizing self-sufficiency and personal responsibility.

THE CULTURE SPECTRUM

Ethics

Moral standards that guide people's behavior.

Shame-based   **Guilt-based**
(seems lawless)   (seems shameless)

▲.................▲.................▲.................▲.................▲

Social respect   **Personal conscience**
(seems shallow)   (seems self-regarding)

▲.................▲.................▲.................▲.................▲

Group Interaction

How people behave and interact with one another.

Social harmony   **Personal freedom**
(seems deferential)   (seems selfish)

▲.................▲.................▲.................▲.................▲

Community-oriented   **Individual-oriented**
(seems like loss of identity)   (seem like overemphasis of self)

▲.................▲.................▲.................▲.................▲

Work and Relationships

How people form and maintain connections with others.

Hierarchical   **Equitable**
(seems oppressive)   (seems disrespectful)

▲.................▲.................▲.................▲.................▲

Relational   **Results-oriented**
(seems like time wasting)   (seems like using people)

▲.................▲.................▲.................▲.................▲

Communication

Methods of conveying important information.

Indirect   **Direct**
(seems disingenuous)   (seems aggressive)

▲................▲................▲................▲................▲

Conflict avoidant   **Assertive engagement**
(seems dishonest)   (seems hostile)

▲................▲................▲................▲................▲

Gathering

How people organize and participate in social events.

Event-oriented   **Time-oriented**
(seems long)   (seems disrespectful)

▲................▲................▲................▲................▲

Celebration

How people express happiness and joy.

Expressive   **Quiet**
(seems loud)   (seems boring)

▲................▲................▲................▲................▲

Age

The importance given to different age groups.

Value elders   **Value youth**
(seems dutiful)   (seems vain)

▲................▲................▲................▲................▲

Money
The role of financial resources in people's lives.

Patronage	Independence
(seems corrupt)	(seems stingy)

▲·····························▲·····························▲·····························▲·····························▲

SCRIPTURAL INTEGRATION

The culture gap between how people relate to these issues is huge! One Christian may express their faith from the far left of the spectrum while another person could express their faith from the far right. Where do the Scriptures fall on this spectrum? Does Jesus endorse one of these directions more than another?

The Scriptures were written within an ancient Near Eastern and Greco-Roman context.[2] The cultural values from the Bible fit more cleanly with the categories toward the left of the culture spectrum. Jesus was born into an honor/shame culture that was collectivist by nature. The common good of all was valued over individual expression. The Hebrew people valued the wisdom of the elderly more than the popularity of the young. First-century Jewish culture was far more event-oriented than time-oriented. Even the Hebrew festivals took place over weeks, with people arriving over periods of days. There was more emphasis on fitting into the system of family or clan instead of standing out as an individual.

Based on the massive differences between the modern West, the ancient Near East, and Greco-Roman culture, it is the responsibility of those in the West to understand the Scriptures from the Eastern world in which they were written. Western Christians who are closer to the right side of the culture spectrum often read the Scriptures from their cultural vantage point. This is a common and dangerous pitfall.

While the cultural contexts of the Scriptures fit more neatly along the left-hand column, the Bible does not mandate that we adopt those values. God has given us freedom in Christ to express our faith from within the cultural values we grew up with. Every Christian must follow the greatest commandment to love God and love neighbor (Matthew 22:37–39) from the cultural locations they inhabit. This will look different depending on our unique cultural background. Every follower of Jesus must display the fruit of the Spirit—love, joy, peace, patience, kindness, self-control, and so on (Galatians 5:22–23)—in their home culture!

This book shows how the Way of Jesus can be followed anywhere in the world, regardless of where you fall on the culture spectrum. Still, we must always consider our cultural blind spots. It is through following Jesus, studying the Scriptures, living in community, entering cross-cultural spaces, and remaining humble that we come to understand how our own culture can blind us to the Way of Jesus.

This culture spectrum tool is meant to help increase your personal awareness of your cultural identity, discern the areas that are more important to you, place yourself within the broader cultural values of the world, and identify any biases you may hold. It is from this foundation that we dive into the Scriptures.

ACKNOWLEDGMENTS

I want to thank my dissertation chair, Dr. Jamie Sanchez, for her leadership, mentorship, and support throughout my academic career at Biola University. From early ideation to field research to the countless supportive edits—I am extremely grateful that she took a chance on me as a student. My faith in Jesus and understanding of culture helped create a foundation for a book such as this.

NOTES

INTRODUCTION

1. To honor the privacy of those who allowed me to share their stories, I have changed the names of individuals throughout the book.

CHAPTER 1

1. Warner Sallman's *Son of Man*, completed in 1924, was acquired to serve as the cover art for the *Covenant Companion*, the official magazine of the Evangelical Covenant Church. The original charcoal painting gained global recognition, having been reproduced more than five hundred million times and displayed worldwide. To further explore the color of Christ, see Edward J. Blum and Paul Harvey, *Color of Christ* (UNC Press Books, 2012).

2. Zora Neale Hurston, *Tell My Horse: Voodoo and Life in Haiti and Jamaica* (Amistad, 2009), loc. 2839, Kindle. First published 1938.

3. For a book that explores the necessity of reading Jesus on his own historical terms, see Jerome H. Neyrey, SJ, *Imagining Jesus in His Own Culture: Creating Scenarios of the Gospel for Contemplative Prayer* (Cascade Books, 2018).

4. For a pivotal book helping Western Christians untangle the Western biases as we understand church history, see Vince L. Bantu, *A Multitude of All Peoples: Engaging Ancient Christianity's Global Identity*, Missiological Engagements (InterVarsity Press, 2020).

CHAPTER 2

1. The challenge for Christians in defining culture is twofold. First, culture relates to absolutely everything! There is nothing that you can think about, do, or say that is outside of culture. Second, the word *culture* does not really show up in the Bible. The closest word we have for *culture* in the Scriptures are the words *cultivate* and *create*. For these reasons, I'll try to keep our definitions of culture and cultural identity simple.

2. In this book, I aim to keep the definition of culture very simple. To dive deeper, see Stephan A. Grunlan and Marvin K. Mayers, *Cultural Anthropology: A Christian Perspective*, 2nd ed. (Zondervan, 1988), 38–50; Brian M. Howell and Jenell Paris,

Introducing Cultural Anthropology: A Christian Perspective (Grand Rapids: Baker Academic, 2019), chap. 2. In this simple definition of culture, I'm accounting for culture as (1) narratives or stories, and (2) what humans cultivate and build in the world. Different academic disciplines emphasize one over the other. Yet we see both happening in the Bible.

To learn more about the academic developments of historic particularism (emphasizing stories/narratives) or structural functionalism (emphasizing structures/systems), see Kenneth J. Guest, *Essentials of Cultural Anthropology: A Toolkit for a Global Age*, 3rd ed. (New York: Norton, 2020), chap. 2.

3. I'm intentionally leaving out religion as an aspect of cultural identity. For the sake of this book, the Christian faith or "religion" is the prism through which we should be understanding the rest of our cultural identity. For this reason, I won't place religion as equal to these other aspects of cultural identity. To explore the place of religion in the study of culture and anthropology, see Rebecca Stein and Philip L. Stein, *The Anthropology of Religion, Magic, and Witchcraft*, 4th ed. (Routledge, 2017).

4. For a deeper reflection on these ten aspects of cultural identity, see the appendix.

5. William Edgar notes that "cultural studies arose within the vacuum created by the loss of a sense of the presence of God in the West." *Created and Creating: A Biblical Theology of Culture* (InterVarsity Press, 2016), 23–24. This book is meant to integrate the scriptural understanding on culture with the best parts of cultural studies.

CHAPTER 3

1. Though this is not covered in the scope of this chapter, it is essential to approach Bible study methods while considering cultural and social location. To explore a range of perspectives, see Gale A. Yee, *Towards an Asian American Biblical Hermeneutics: An Intersectional Anthology* (Cascade Books, 2021); Francisco Lozada, *A Latino/a Biblical Hermeneutics: Problematics, Objectives, Strategies*, Semeia Studies 68 (SBL Press, 2017); Hugh R. Page Jr. et al., eds., *The Africana Bible: Reading Israel's Scriptures from Africa and the African Diaspora* (Fortress, 2009); Leroy Barber and Jess Bielman, *A Hermeneutic of Liberation: Reading Scripture From the Margins* (Voices Publishing, 2023); Jeffrey P. Greenman and Gene L. Green, eds., *Global Theology in Evangelical Perspective: Exploring the Contextual Nature of Theology and Mission*, Wheaton Theology Conference Series (IVP Academic, 2021).

2. For a good critique on a Western reading of Scripture, see E. Randolph Richards and Brandon J. O'Brien, *Misreading Scripture with Western Eyes: Removing Cultural Blinders to Better Understand the Bible* (IVP, 2012).

3. "Biblical hermeneutics" refers to the interpretation of Scripture. Your hermeneutic is the way you decide how to find meaning in the Bible. Everyone has a hermeneutic whether they know it or not. The story I shared about my Bible study with Adam is an example of a bad hermeneutic.

4. Brandon D. Smith and Everett Berry highlight nine examples from the Old Testament where Jesus unlocks the passages in focus. See *They Spoke of Me: How Jesus Unlocks the Old Testament* (Rainer Publishing, 2018).

5. For a great practical devotional resource exploring Jesus' centrality in the Old Testament, see Nancy Guthrie, *The One-Year Book of Discovering Jesus in the Old Testament* (Tyndale, 2010). Another practical book exploring the centrality of Jesus in

the Old Testament is David Murray, *Jesus on Every Page: 10 Simple Ways to Seek and Find Christ in the Old Testament* (Thomas Nelson, 2013).

6. To explore this further, see Douglas Van Dorn, *Christ in the Old Testament: Promised, Patterned, and Present*, Christ in All Scripture 5 (Waters of Creation Publishing, 2019); Edmund P. Clowney, *The Unfolding Mystery: Discovering Christ in the Old Testament*, 2nd. ed. (P&R Publishing, 2013); Dennis E. Johnson, *Walking with Jesus through His Word: Discovering Christ in All the Scriptures* (P&R Publishing, 2015).

7. For more on this point, see Christopher J. H. Wright, *How to Preach and Teach the Old Testament for All Its Worth* (Zondervan Academic, 2016).

8. For more resources exploring the topic of this chapter, see Chad Bird, *The Christ Key: Unlocking the Centrality of Christ in the Old Testament* (1517 Publishing, 2021).

CHAPTER 4

1. Special thanks to the President of Eternity Bible College Ernesto Duke for offering theological and editorial support for many of the Old Testament chapters.

2. For more on the concept of the imago Dei, see John F. Kilner, *Dignity and Destiny: Humanity in the Image of God* (Grand Rapids: Eerdmans, 2015); International Commission for Anglican-Orthodox Theological Dialogue, *In the Image and Likeness of God: A Hope-Filled Anthropology—The Buffalo Statement* (London: Anglican Communion Office, 2015).

CHAPTER 5

1. For a good resource exploring the Table of Nations, see J. Daniel Hays, *From Every People and Nation: A Biblical Theology of Race*, New Studies in Biblical Theology 14 (InterVarsity Press, 2016), 56–60.

2. Steven M. Bryan, *Cultural Identity and the Purposes of God: A Biblical Theology of Ethnicity, Nationality, and Race* (Crossway, 2022), 42.

CHAPTER 6

1. New Testament scholars believe that many of Jesus' conversations in the New Testament were multilingual, some in Greek, some in Hebrew and probably some in Aramaic. Finally, as followers of Jesus, we believe that through the new covenant, Jesus is making all things good and right. We see that on the day of Pentecost, the Spirit did not give the gift to all the hearers to understand the language of the apostles, but gave the apostles the gifts of diverse language. In Revelation, people of all tribes, tongues (languages), and nations come to worship the Lamb in cultural diversity.

CHAPTER 8

1. Hemchand Gossai, *Power and Marginality in the Abraham Narrative*, 2nd ed., Princeton Theological Monograph Series Book 130 (Pickwick, 1995).

2. An important book exploring Old Testament violence from the cultural perspective of Central and South America is Susanne Scholz, *La Violencia and the Hebrew Bible: The Politics and Histories of Biblical Hermeneutics on the American Continent*, Semeia Studies 82 (SBL Press, 2016).

3. For a deeper treatment of the conquest narrative that integrates cultural studies with biblical scholarship, see Steven M. Bryan, *Cultural Identity and the Purposes of God:*

   A Biblical Theology of Ethnicity, Nationality, and Race (Crossway, 2022), 114–41. Kindle Edition.

  4. For more on this, see Christopher J. H. Wright, *Knowing Jesus through the Old Testament*, 2nd. ed. (InterVarsity Press, 2014).

CHAPTER 11

  1. Chandra Crane, *Mixed Blessing: Embracing the Fullness of Your Multiethnic Identity* (InterVarsity Press, 2020), 93.

  2. Gosnell L. Yorke, "Patois Bible in Pan-African and Pan-Caribbean Context," *Jamaica Gleaner*, June 29, 2008, http://old.jamaica-gleaner.com/gleaner/20080629/lead/lead8.html; quoted in Delano Palmer and Samantha Mosha, *New Testament Theology: Identity and I-deology* (Extra Mile Innovators, 2019), 35.

  3. N. T. Wright and Michael F. Bird, *The New Testament in Its World: An Introduction to the History, Literature, and Theology of the First Christians* (Zondervan Academic, 2019), 111–12.

CHAPTER 12

  1. For more on the Luke 4 vision of Jubilee, see Bryan R. Dyer, "Good News to the Poor: Social Upheaval, Strong Warnings and Sincere Giving in Luke-Acts," in *The Bible and Social Justice: Old Testament and New Testament Foundations for the Church's Urgent Call*, ed. Cynthia Long Westfall and Bryan R. Dyer (Wipf & Stock, 2016), 118–39; Joel B. Green, *The Theology of the Gospel of Luke* (Cambridge University Press, 1995), 76–101; and André Trocmé, *Jesus and the Nonviolent Revolution* (Plough, 2014).

CHAPTER 14

  1. Nehemiah Adams, *The Life of John Eliot: An Account of the Early Missionary Efforts among the Indians of New England* (n.p., 1870), 43.

  2. Ruth Tucker, *From Jerusalem to Irian Jaya: A Biographical History of Christian Missions* (Zondervan Academic, 2004), 77.

CHAPTER 16

  1. See Stephen R. Tertullian Haynes, *Noah's Curse: The Biblical Justification of American Slavery* (Oxford University Press, 2002).

  2. For more on these developments, see Joe R. Feagin, *The White Racial Frame: Centuries of Racial Framing and Counter-Framing* (Taylor and Francis, 2009), 39–58.

  3. David Hume, *On National Characters* (1754); quoted in Ali Rattansi, *Racism: A Very Short Introduction* (OUP Oxford, 2007), 27.

  4. For more on these developments, see Willie James Jennings, *The Christian Imagination: Theology and the Origins of Race* (Yale University Press, 2011).

  5. See Christian Smith and Michael O. Emerson, *Divided by Faith: Evangelical Religion and the Problem of Race in America* (Oxford University Press, 2000); Colin Kidd, *The Forging of Races: Race and Scripture in the Protestant Atlantic World, 1600–2000* (Cambridge University Press, 2006); J. Kameron Carter, *Race: A Theological Account* (Oxford University Press, 2008).

CHAPTER 17

1. For instance, during the Feast of Tabernacles (Sukkot), people carried palm branches as part of the celebration, commemorating the Israelites' journey through the wilderness and God's provision and victory over their hardships (Leviticus 23:40).

APPENDIX

1. This tool makes no value judgment on what has been presented on the left or the right of the spectrum. This means that even though English-language texts are read from left to right, you are not supposed to consider what you read first as the right way to personally identify.

2. A good book exploring the various ways that people understand the gospel based on some of the values highlighted in the spectrum is Jayson Georges, *The 3D Gospel: Ministry in Guilt, Shame, and Fear Cultures* (Timē Press, 2014).

THE AUTHOR

J. W. BUCK is a church planter, filmmaker, teacher, and faith-based entrepreneur. He has a BA in biblical studies, an MA in ministry, and a PhD in intercultural studies. His doctoral work focuses on the problem of racial violence. In 2010, Buck planted a church in Los Angeles called Antioch City Church. In 2019, he helped start a Jesus-centered organization  called Pax. Buck is the author of *Everyday Activism: Following 7 Practices of Jesus to Create a Just World* (Baker, 2022). He is married to Sarswatie and father to Aahana, Anaia, and Azariah. They live in southwest Tucson, Arizona.